Based on the TV series episodes by
**MAN OF ACTION, JAY FAERBER,
PAUL GIACOPPO, JACOB SEMAHN
& JOE FALLON**

Adapted by
JOE CARAMAGNA
with special thanks to
Marvel Animation & Product Factory

Editor
SEBASTIAN GIRNER

Consulting Editor
JON MOISAN

Senior Editor
MARK PANICCIA

Collection Editor
ALEX STARBUCK

Assistant Editor
SARAH BRUNSTAD

Editors, Special Projects
**JENNIFER GRÜNWALD
& MARK D. BEAZLEY**

Senior Editor, Special Projects
JEFF YOUNGQUIST

SVP Print, Sales & Marketing
DAVID GABRIEL
Book Design
NELSON RIBEIRO

Editor In Chief
AXEL ALONSO

Chief Creative Officer
JOE QUESADA

Publisher
DAN BUCKLEY

Executive Producer
ALAN FINE

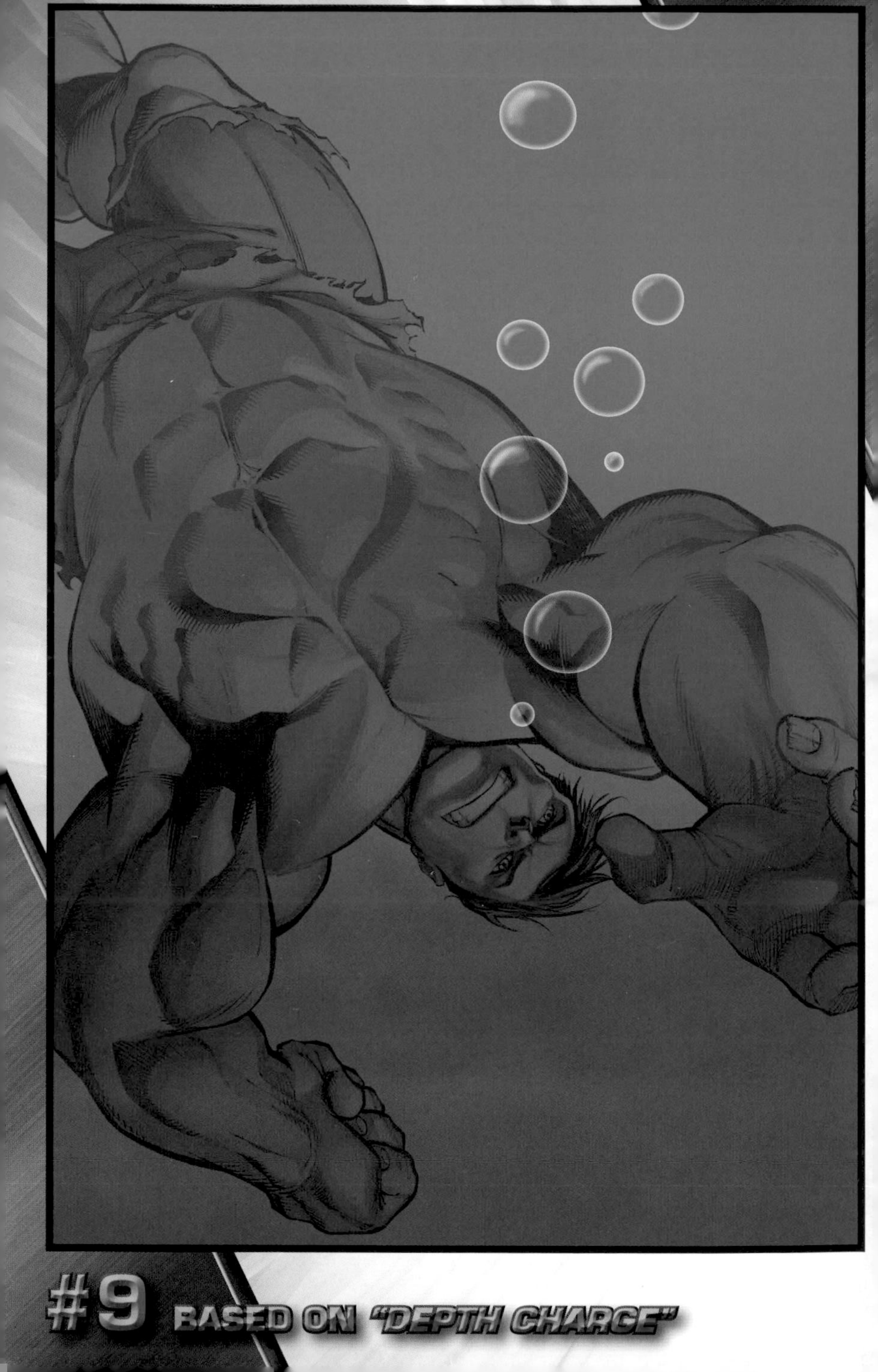

#9 BASED ON "DEPTH CHARGE"

MARVEL UNIVERSE AVENGERS ASSEMBLE VOL. 3. Contains material originally published in magazine form as MARVEL UNIVERSE AVENGERS ASSEMBLE #9-12. First printing 2014. ISBN# 978-0-7851-8881-0. Published by MARVEL WORLDWIDE, INC., a subsidiary of MARVEL ENTERTAINMENT, LLC. OFFICE OF PUBLICATION: 135 West 50th Street, New York, NY 10020. Copyright © 2014 Marvel Characters, Inc. All rights reserved. All characters featured in this issue and the distinctive names and likenesses thereof, and all related indicia are trademarks of Marvel Characters, Inc. No similarity between any of the names, characters, persons, and/or institutions in this magazine with those of any living or dead person or institution is intended, and any such similarity which may exist is purely coincidental. **Printed in the U.S.A.** ALAN FINE, EVP - Office of the President, Marvel Worldwide, Inc. and EVP & CMO Marvel Characters B.V.; DAN BUCKLEY, Publisher & President - Print, Animation & Digital Divisions; JOE QUESADA, Chief Creative Officer; TOM BREVOORT, SVP of Publishing; DAVID BOGART, SVP of Operations & Procurement, Publishing; C.B. CEBULSKI, SVP of Creator & Content Development; DAVID GABRIEL, SVP Print, Sales & Marketing; JIM O'KEEFE, VP of Operations & Logistics; DAN CARR, Executive Director of Publishing Technology; SUSAN CRESPI, Editorial Operations Manager; ALEX MORALES, Publishing Operations Manager; STAN LEE, Chairman Emeritus. For information regarding advertising in Marvel Comics or on Marvel.com, please contact Niza Disla, Director of Marvel Partnerships, at ndisla@marvel.com. For Marvel subscription inquiries, please call 800-217-9158. **Manufactured between 9/19/2014 and 10/27/2014 by SHERIDAN BOOKS, INC., CHELSEA, MI, USA.**

10 9 8 7 6 5 4 3 2 1

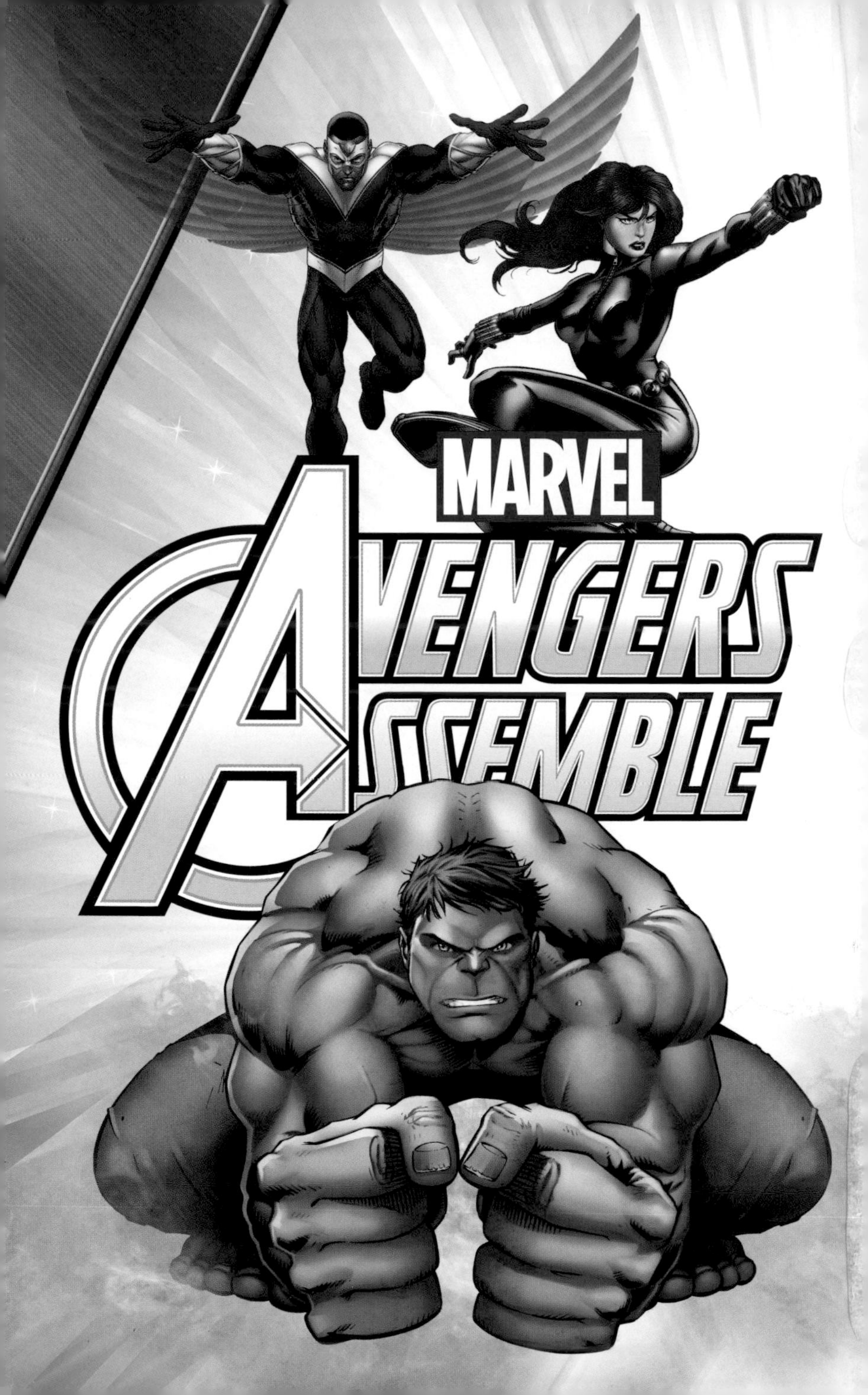
MARVEL
AVENGERS
ASSEMBLE

MARVEL AVENGERS ASSEMBLE

IRON MAN

CAPTAIN AMERICA

THOR

BLACK WIDOW

HAWKEYE

HULK

FALCON

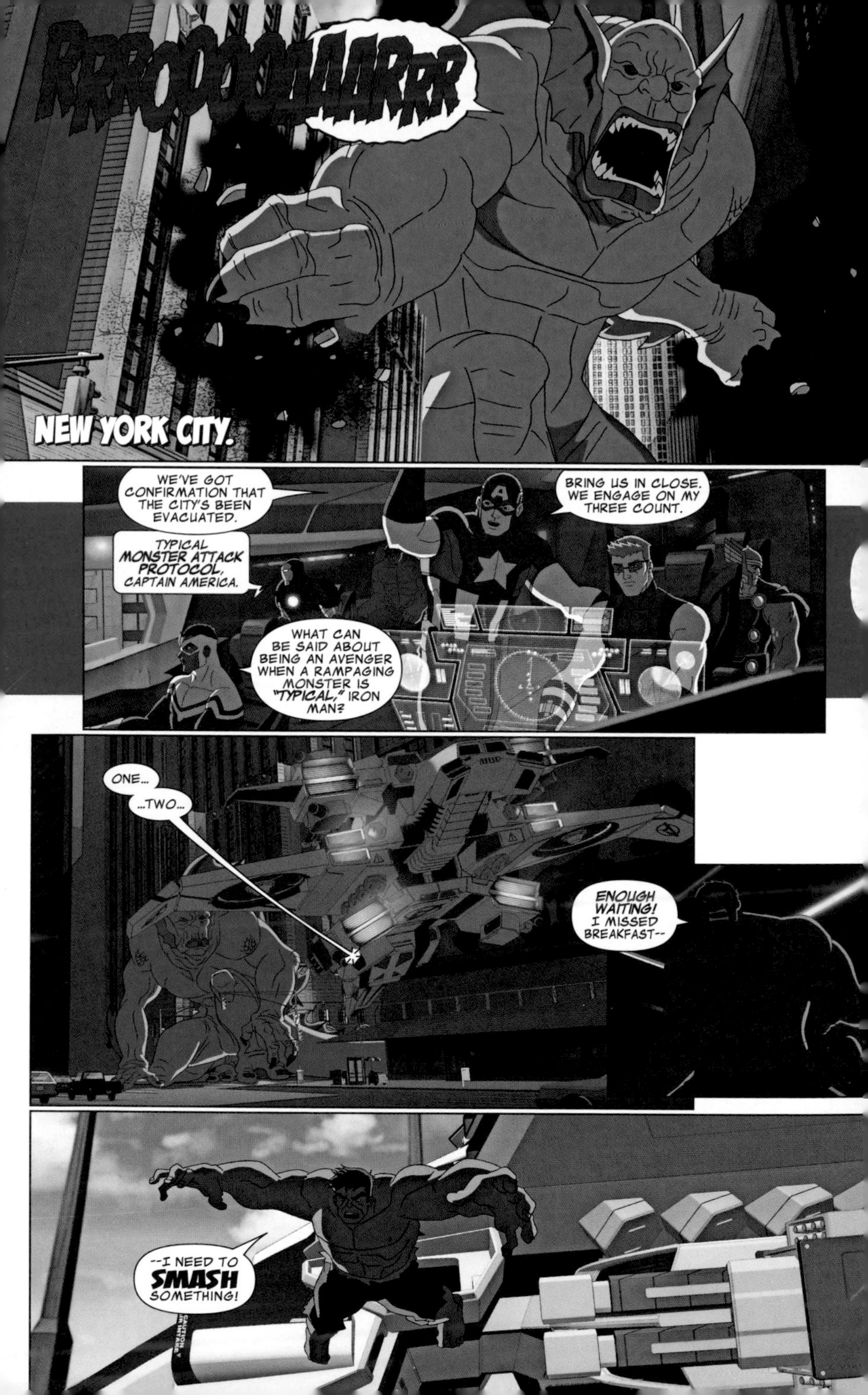
RRRROOOOAARRR
NEW YORK CITY.
WE'VE GOT CONFIRMATION THAT THE CITY'S BEEN EVACUATED.
TYPICAL MONSTER ATTACK PROTOCOL, CAPTAIN AMERICA.
BRING US IN CLOSE. WE ENGAGE ON MY THREE COUNT.
WHAT CAN BE SAID ABOUT BEING AN AVENGER WHEN A RAMPAGING MONSTER IS "TYPICAL," IRON MAN?
ONE...
...TWO...
ENOUGH WAITING! I MISSED BREAKFAST--
--I NEED TO SMASH SOMETHING!

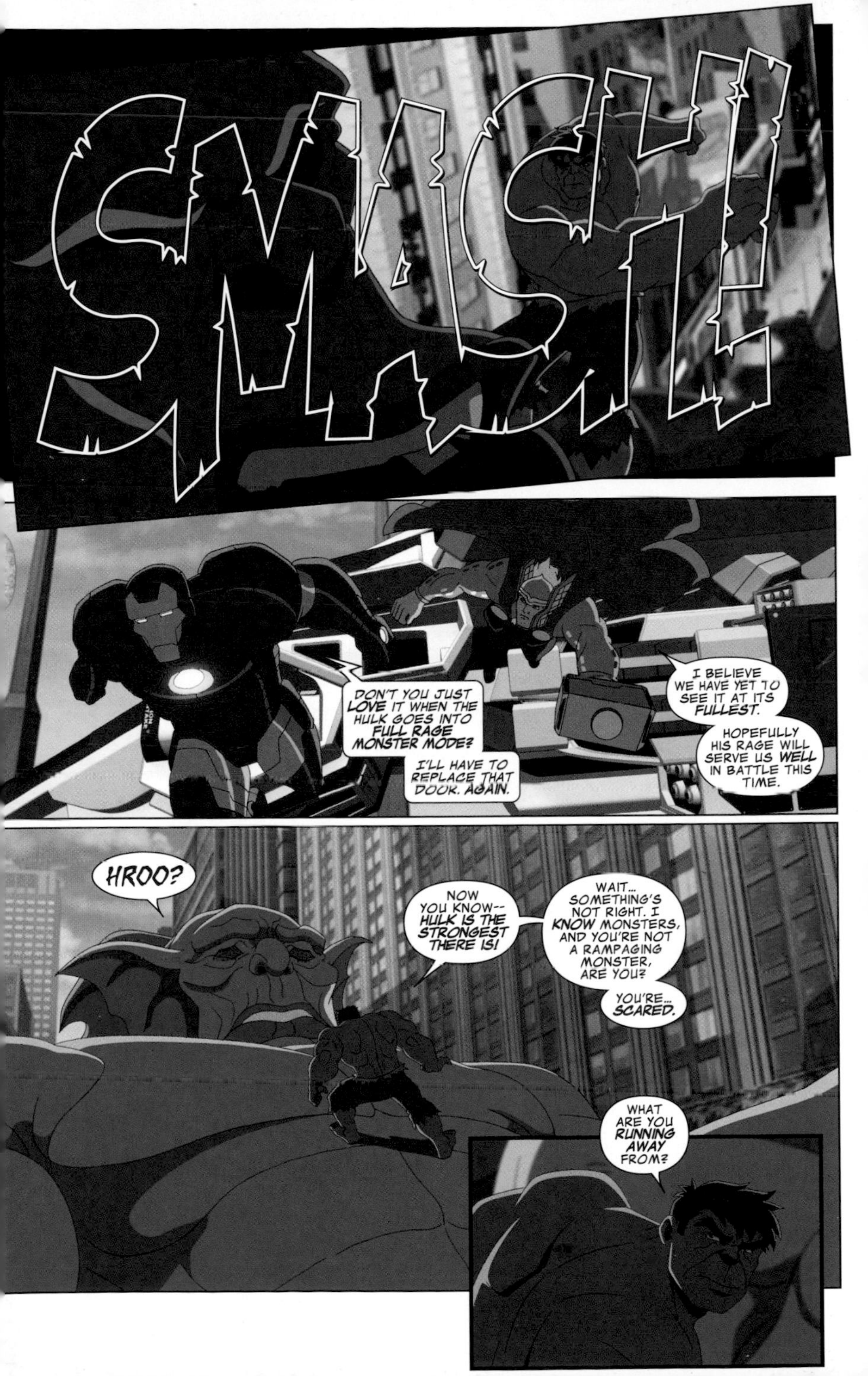
SMASH!
DON'T YOU JUST LOVE IT WHEN THE HULK GOES INTO FULL RAGE MONSTER MODE?
I'LL HAVE TO REPLACE THAT DOOR. AGAIN.
I BELIEVE WE HAVE YET TO SEE IT AT ITS FULLEST.
HOPEFULLY HIS RAGE WILL SERVE US WELL IN BATTLE THIS TIME.
HROO?
NOW YOU KNOW-- HULK IS THE STRONGEST THERE IS!
WAIT... SOMETHING'S NOT RIGHT. I KNOW MONSTERS, AND YOU'RE NOT A RAMPAGING MONSTER, ARE YOU?
YOU'RE... SCARED.
WHAT ARE YOU RUNNING AWAY FROM?

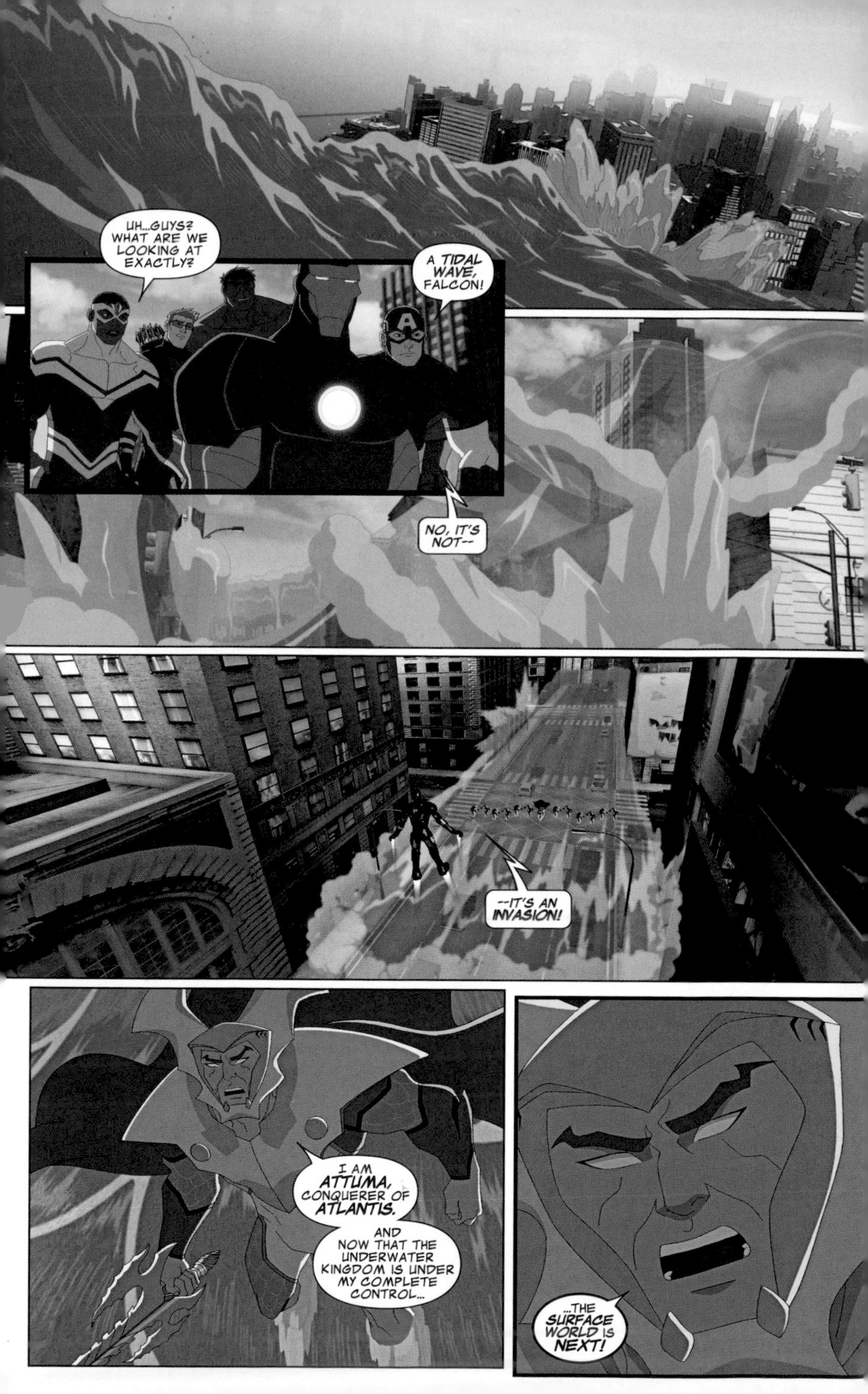
UH...GUYS? WHAT ARE WE LOOKING AT EXACTLY?
A TIDAL WAVE, FALCON!
NO, IT'S NOT--
--IT'S AN INVASION!
I AM ATTUMA, CONQUERER OF ATLANTIS.
AND NOW THAT THE UNDERWATER KINGDOM IS UNDER MY COMPLETE CONTROL...
...THE SURFACE WORLD IS NEXT!

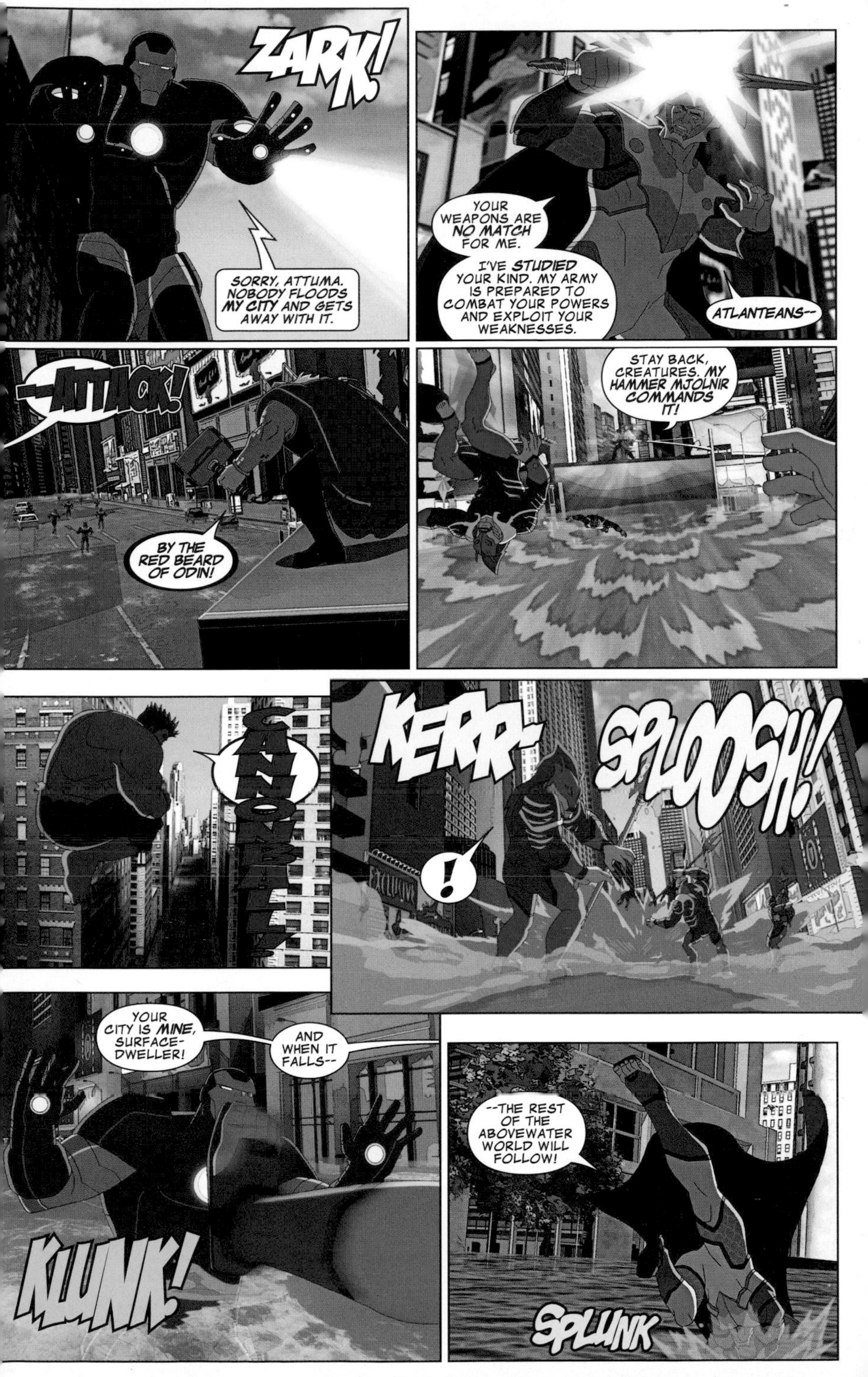
ZARK!
SORRY, ATTUMA. NOBODY FLOODS MY CITY AND GETS AWAY WITH IT.
YOUR WEAPONS ARE NO MATCH FOR ME.
I'VE STUDIED YOUR KIND. MY ARMY IS PREPARED TO COMBAT YOUR POWERS AND EXPLOIT YOUR WEAKNESSES.
ATLANTEANS--
--ATTACK!
BY THE RED BEARD OF ODIN!
STAY BACK, CREATURES. MY HAMMER MJOLNIR COMMANDS IT!
CANNONBALL
KERR-
SPLOOSH!!
!
YOUR CITY IS MINE, SURFACE-DWELLER!
AND WHEN IT FALLS--
KLUNK!
--THE REST OF THE ABOVEWATER WORLD WILL FOLLOW!
SPLUNK

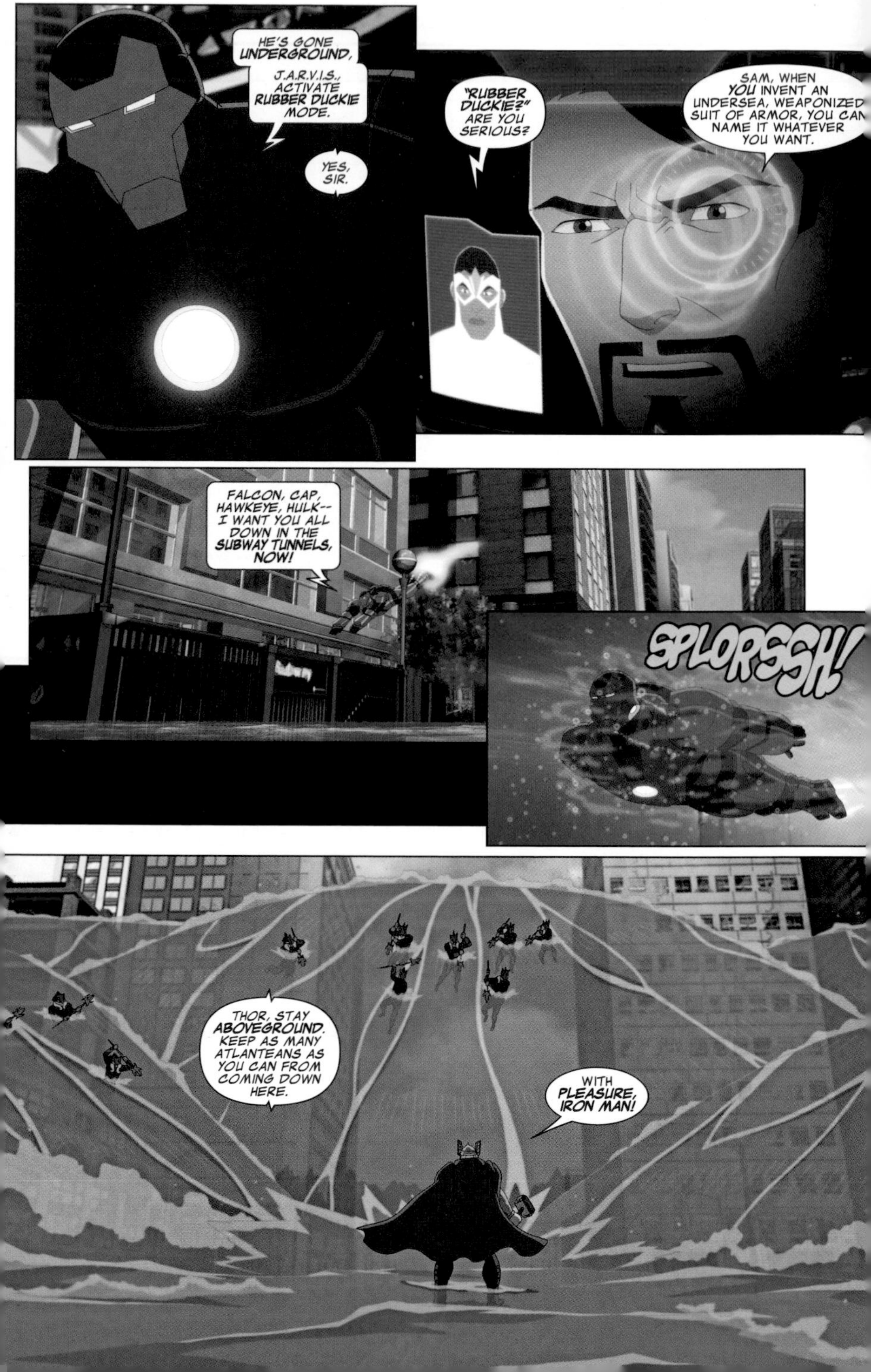
HE'S GONE UNDERGROUND,
J.A.R.V.I.S., ACTIVATE RUBBER DUCKIE MODE.
YES, SIR.
"RUBBER DUCKIE?" ARE YOU SERIOUS?
SAM, WHEN YOU INVENT AN UNDERSEA, WEAPONIZED SUIT OF ARMOR, YOU CAN NAME IT WHATEVER YOU WANT.
FALCON, CAP, HAWKEYE, HULK-- I WANT YOU ALL DOWN IN THE SUBWAY TUNNELS, NOW!
SPLORSSH!
THOR, STAY ABOVEGROUND. KEEP AS MANY ATLANTEANS AS YOU CAN FROM COMING DOWN HERE.
WITH PLEASURE, IRON MAN!

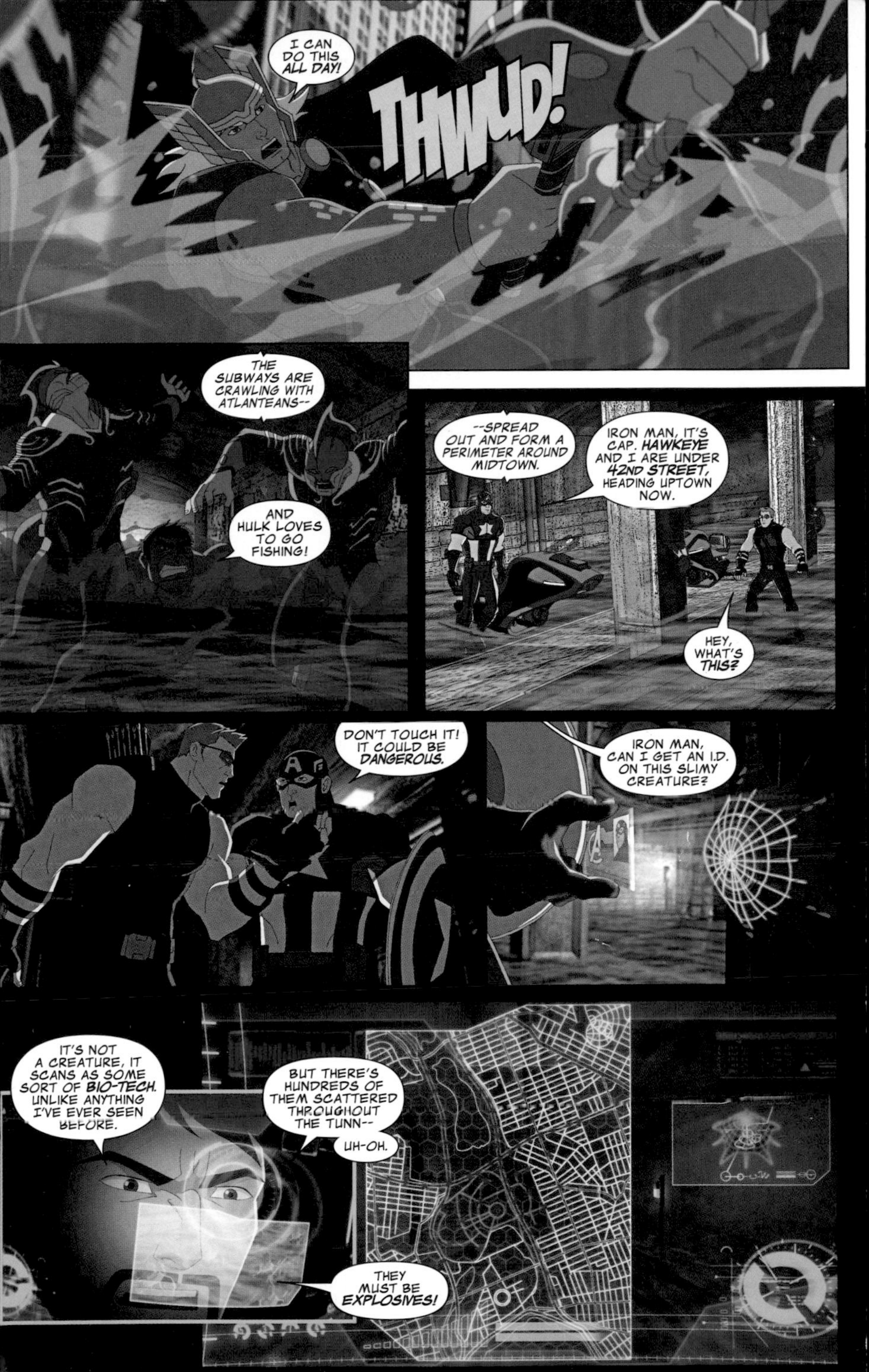
I CAN DO THIS ALL DAY!
THWUD!
THE SUBWAYS ARE CRAWLING WITH ATLANTEANS--
AND HULK LOVES TO GO FISHING!
--SPREAD OUT AND FORM A PERIMETER AROUND MIDTOWN.
IRON MAN, IT'S CAP. HAWKEYE AND I ARE UNDER 42ND STREET, HEADING UPTOWN NOW.
HEY, WHAT'S THIS?
DON'T TOUCH IT! IT COULD BE DANGEROUS.
IRON MAN, CAN I GET AN I.D. ON THIS SLIMY CREATURE?
IT'S NOT A CREATURE, IT SCANS AS SOME SORT OF BIO-TECH. UNLIKE ANYTHING I'VE EVER SEEN BEFORE.
BUT THERE'S HUNDREDS OF THEM SCATTERED THROUGHOUT THE TUNN--
UH-OH.
THEY MUST BE EXPLOSIVES!

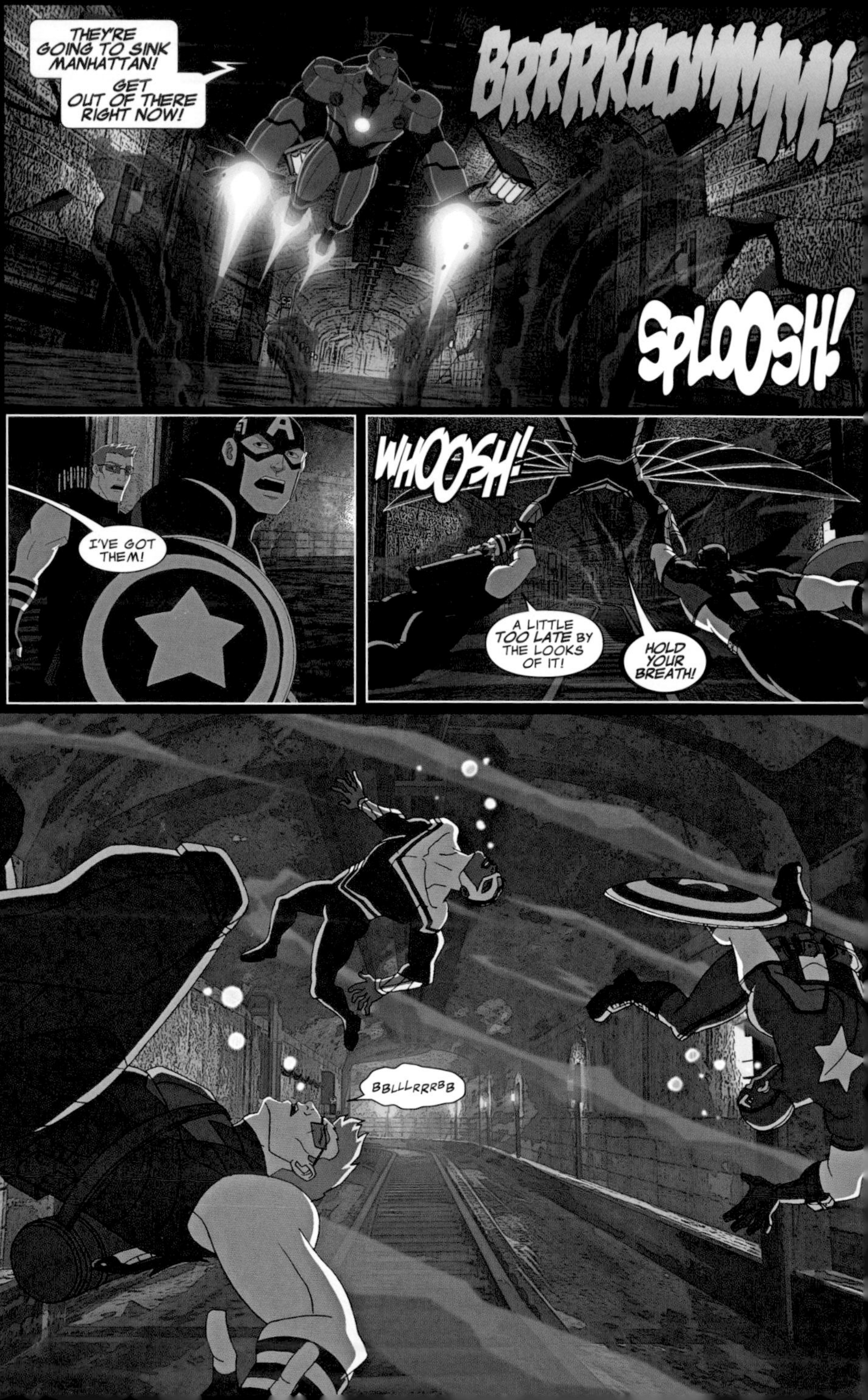
THEY'RE GOING TO SINK MANHATTAN! GET OUT OF THERE RIGHT NOW!
BRRRKOOMMM!
SPLOOSH!
I'VE GOT THEM!
WHOOSH!
A LITTLE TOO LATE BY THE LOOKS OF IT!
HOLD YOUR BREATH!
BBLLLRRRBB

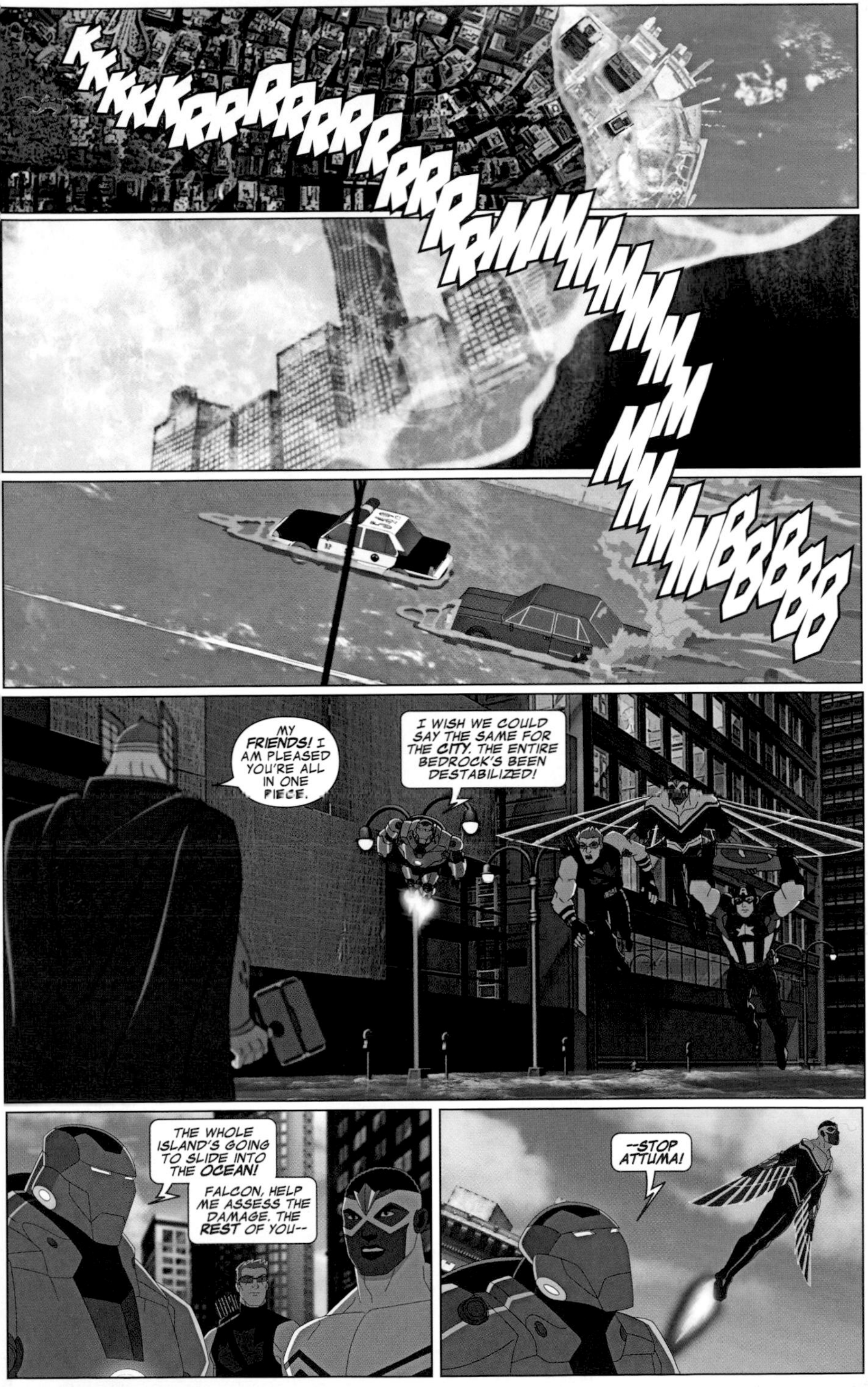
KKKKRRRRRRRRRRRRRMMMMMMMMMMMMMMMMBBBBB
MY FRIENDS! I AM PLEASED YOU'RE ALL IN ONE PIECE.
I WISH WE COULD SAY THE SAME FOR THE CITY. THE ENTIRE BEDROCK'S BEEN DESTABILIZED!
THE WHOLE ISLAND'S GOING TO SLIDE INTO THE OCEAN!
FALCON, HELP ME ASSESS THE DAMAGE. THE REST OF YOU--
--STOP ATTUMA!

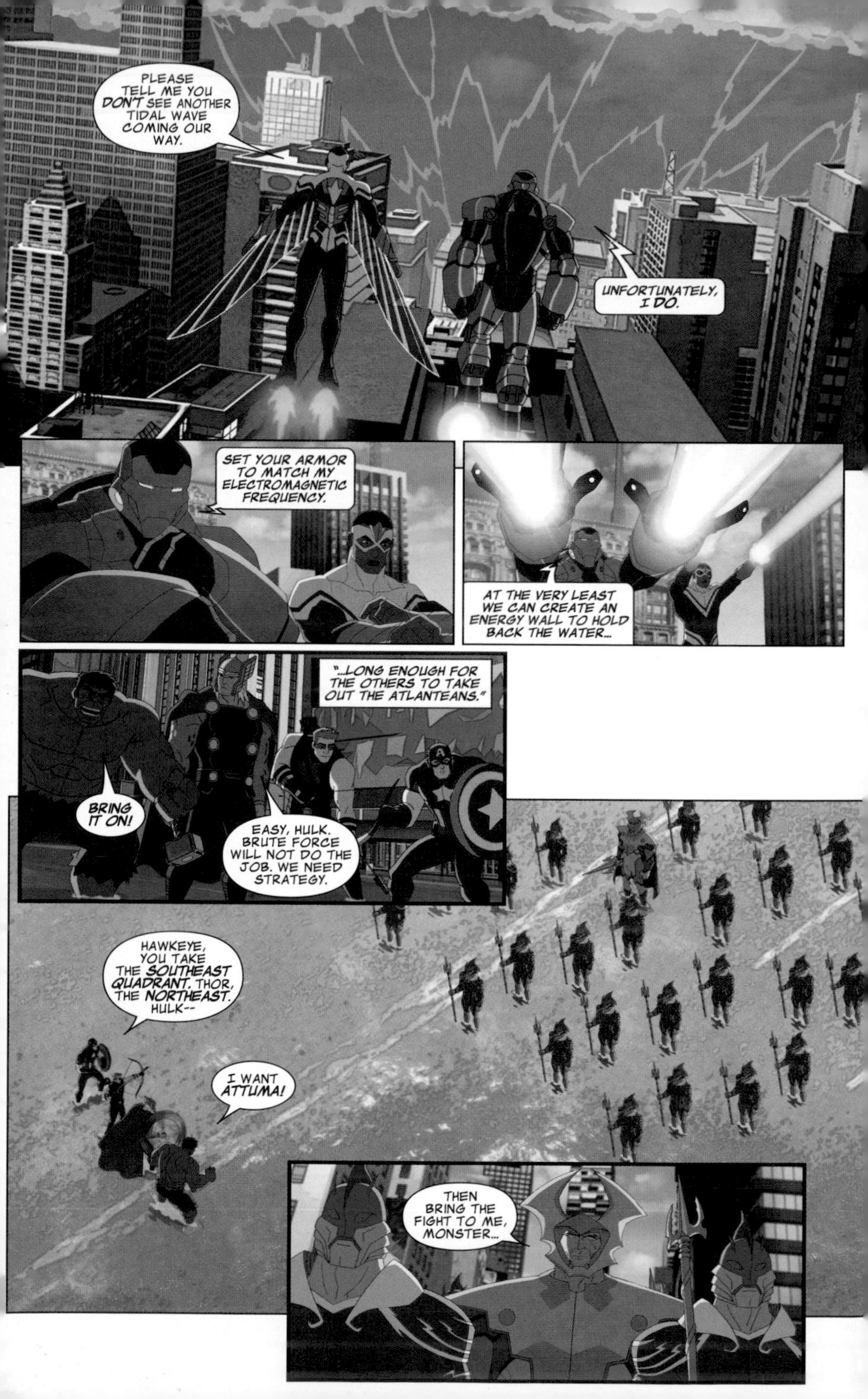
PLEASE TELL ME YOU DON'T SEE ANOTHER TIDAL WAVE COMING OUR WAY.
UNFORTUNATELY, I DO.
SET YOUR ARMOR TO MATCH MY ELECTROMAGNETIC FREQUENCY.
AT THE VERY LEAST WE CAN CREATE AN ENERGY WALL TO HOLD BACK THE WATER...
"...LONG ENOUGH FOR THE OTHERS TO TAKE OUT THE ATLANTEANS."
BRING IT ON!
EASY, HULK. BRUTE FORCE WILL NOT DO THE JOB. WE NEED STRATEGY.
HAWKEYE, YOU TAKE THE SOUTHEAST QUADRANT. THOR, THE NORTHEAST. HULK--
I WANT ATTUMA!
THEN BRING THE FIGHT TO ME, MONSTER...

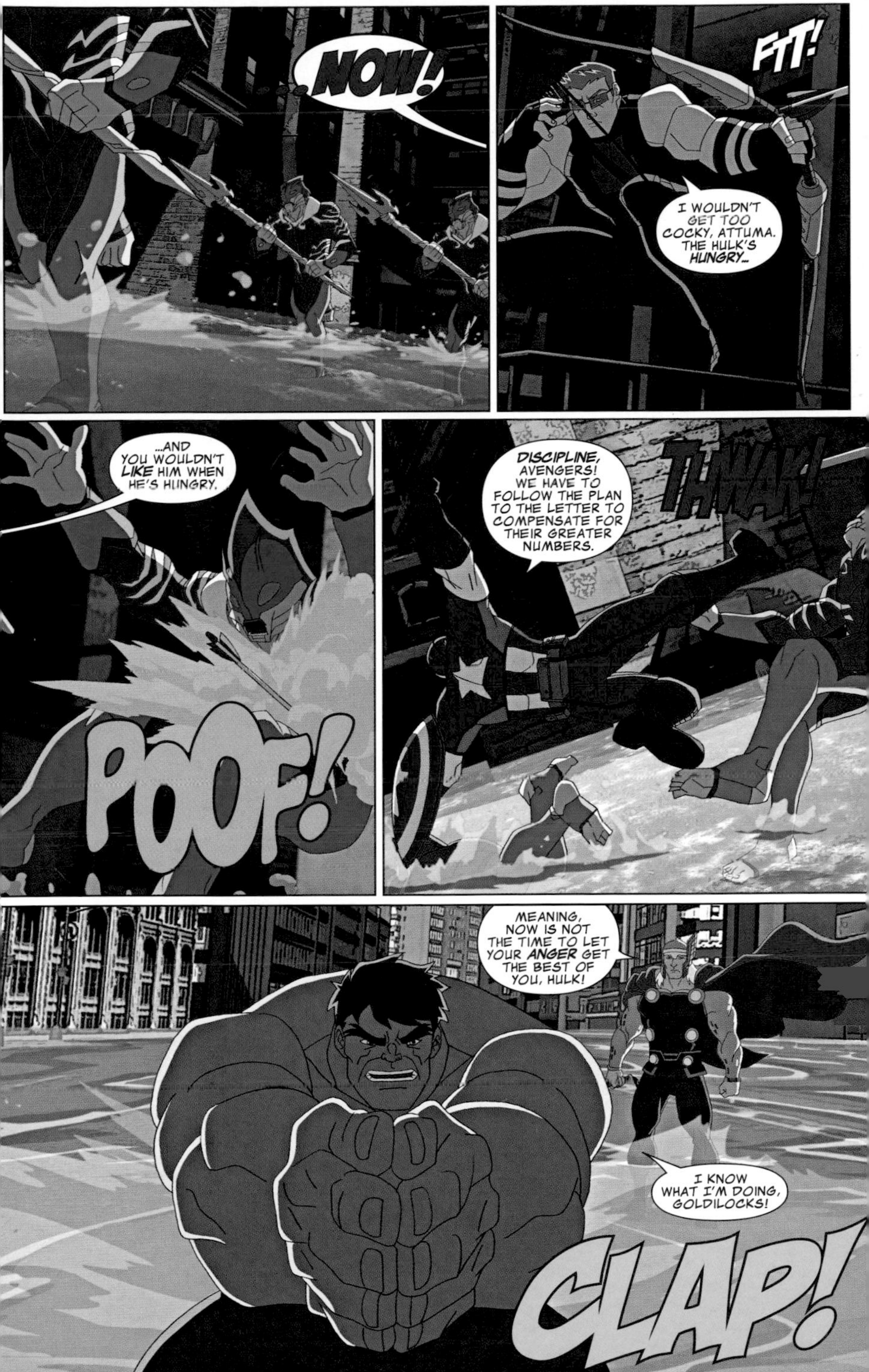
...NOW!
FTT!
I WOULDN'T GET TOO COCKY, ATTUMA. THE HULK'S HUNGRY...
...AND YOU WOULDN'T LIKE HIM WHEN HE'S HUNGRY.
POOF!
DISCIPLINE, AVENGERS! WE HAVE TO FOLLOW THE PLAN TO THE LETTER TO COMPENSATE FOR THEIR GREATER NUMBERS.
THWAK!
MEANING, NOW IS NOT THE TIME TO LET YOUR ANGER GET THE BEST OF YOU, HULK!
I KNOW WHAT I'M DOING, GOLDILOCKS!
CLAP!

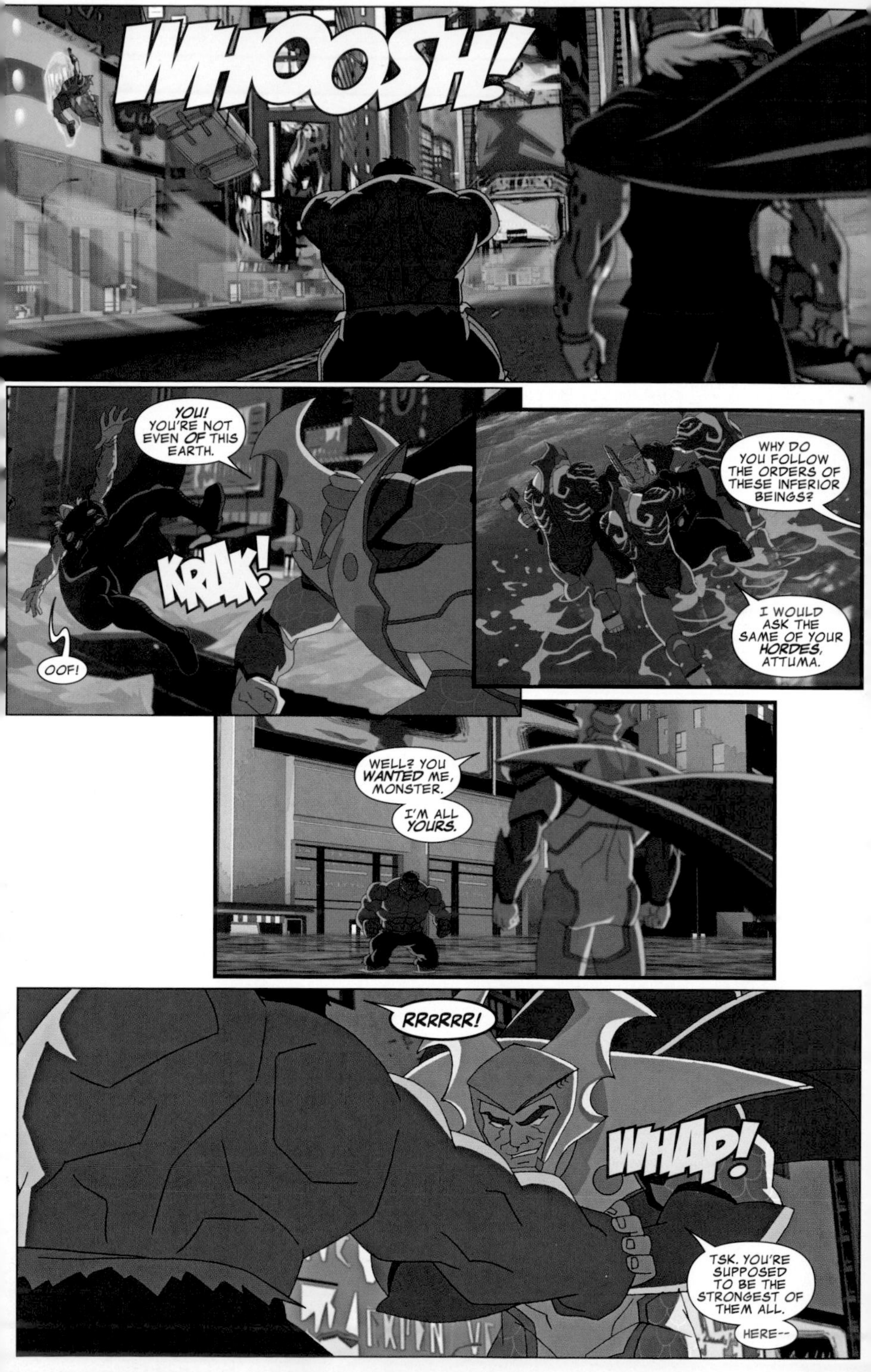
WHOOSH!
YOU! YOU'RE NOT EVEN OF THIS EARTH.
KRAK!
OOF!
WHY DO YOU FOLLOW THE ORDERS OF THESE INFERIOR BEINGS?
I WOULD ASK THE SAME OF YOUR HORDES, ATTUMA.
WELL? YOU WANTED ME, MONSTER.
I'M ALL YOURS.
RRRRRR!
WHAP!
TSK. YOU'RE SUPPOSED TO BE THE STRONGEST OF THEM ALL.
HERE--

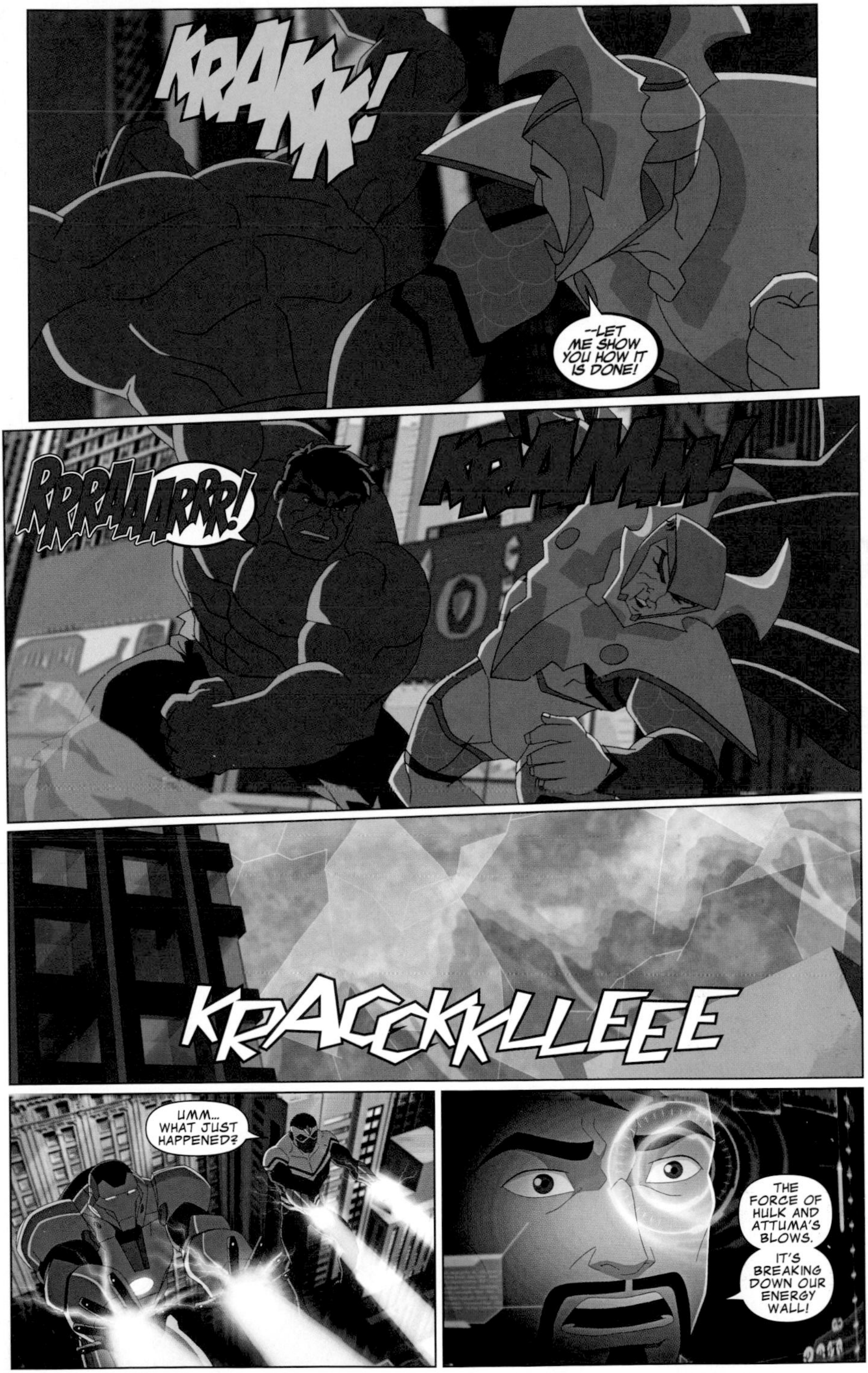
KRAKK!
--LET ME SHOW YOU HOW IT IS DONE!
RRRAAAARRR!
KRAMM!
KRACKKLLEEE
UMM... WHAT JUST HAPPENED?
THE FORCE OF HULK AND ATTUMA'S BLOWS.
IT'S BREAKING DOWN OUR ENERGY WALL!

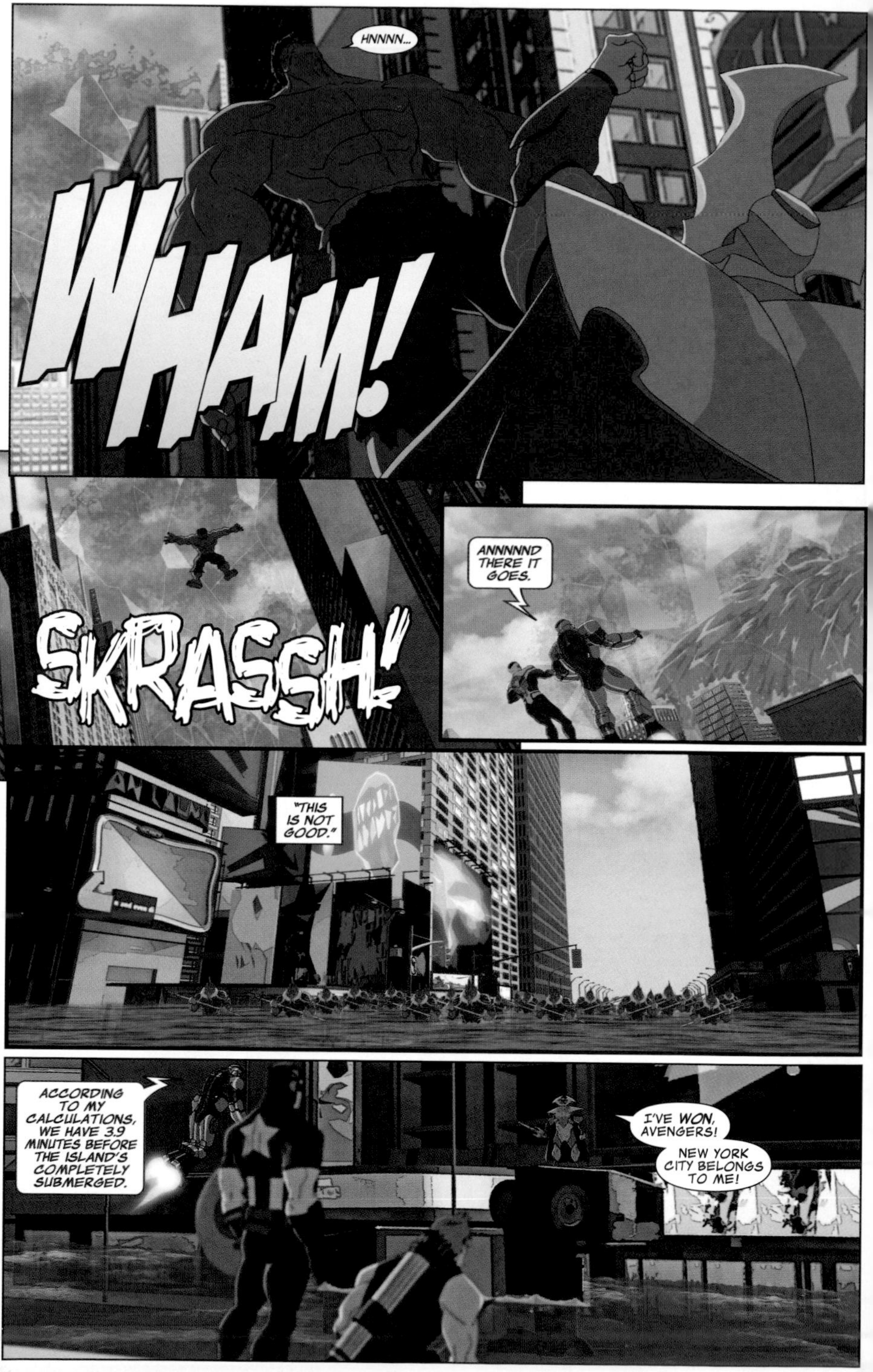
HNNNN...
WHAM!
SKRASSH!
ANNNNND THERE IT GOES.
"THIS IS NOT GOOD."
ACCORDING TO MY CALCULATIONS, WE HAVE 3.9 MINUTES BEFORE THE ISLAND'S COMPLETELY SUBMERGED.
I'VE WON, AVENGERS!
NEW YORK CITY BELONGS TO ME!

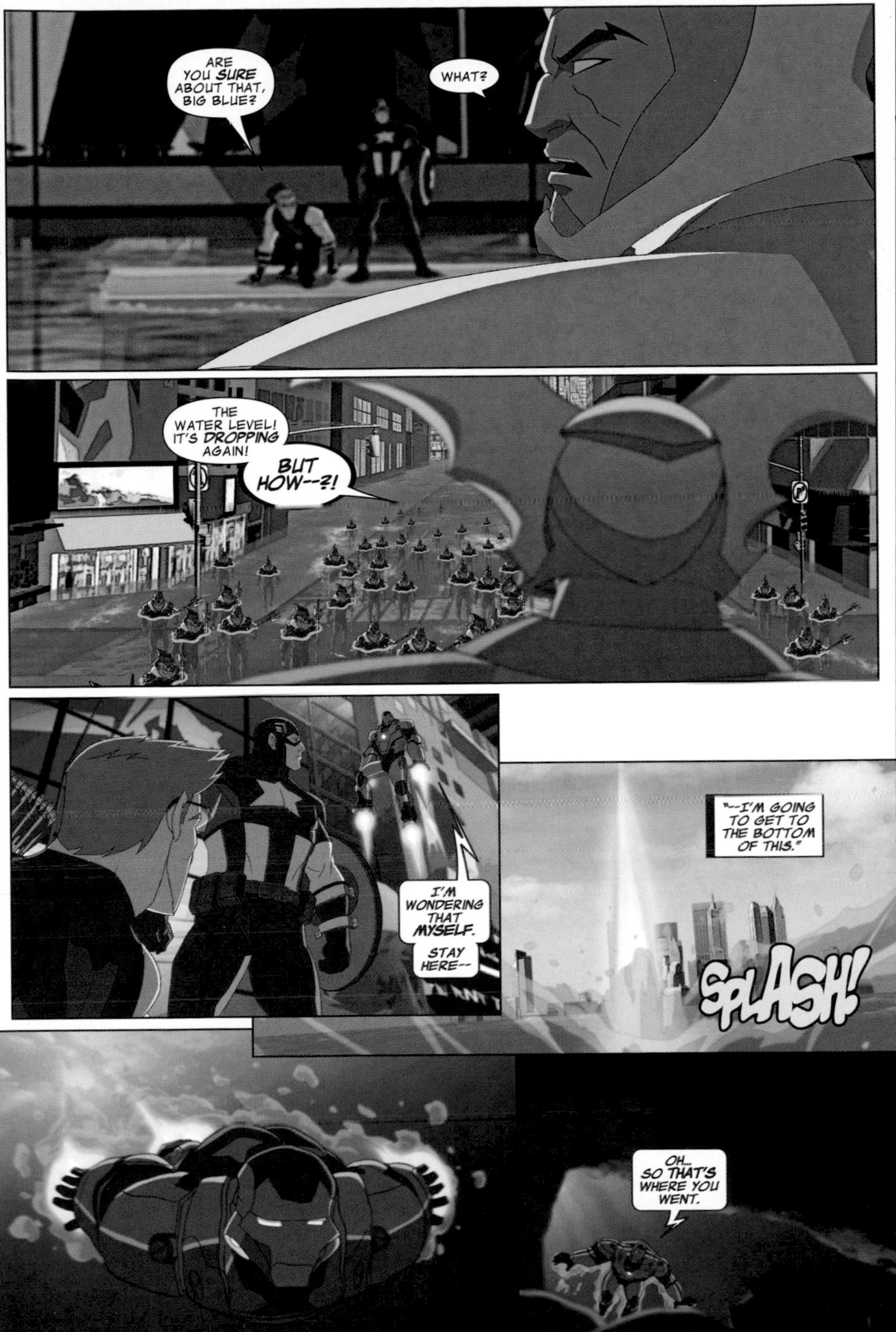
ARE YOU SURE ABOUT THAT, BIG BLUE?
WHAT?
THE WATER LEVEL! IT'S DROPPING AGAIN!
BUT HOW--?!
I'M WONDERING THAT MYSELF.
STAY HERE--
"--I'M GOING TO GET TO THE BOTTOM OF THIS."
SPLASH!
OH... SO THAT'S WHERE YOU WENT.

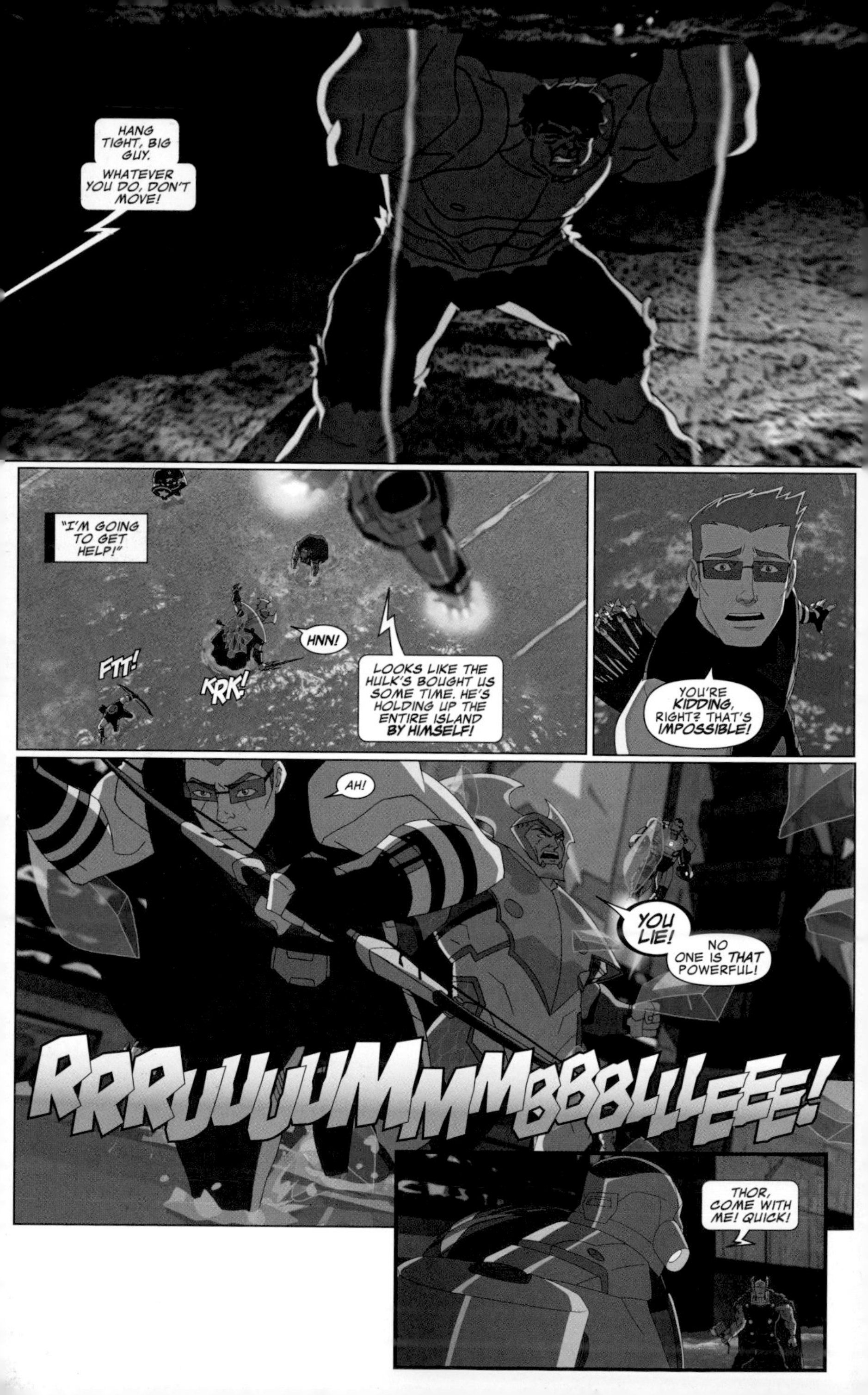
HANG TIGHT, BIG GUY.
WHATEVER YOU DO, DON'T MOVE!
"I'M GOING TO GET HELP!"
HNN!
FTT!
KRK!
LOOKS LIKE THE HULK'S BOUGHT US SOME TIME. HE'S HOLDING UP THE ENTIRE ISLAND BY HIMSELF!
YOU'RE KIDDING, RIGHT? THAT'S IMPOSSIBLE!
AH!
YOU LIE!
NO ONE IS THAT POWERFUL!
RRRUUUUMMMBBBLLLEEE!
THOR, COME WITH ME! QUICK!

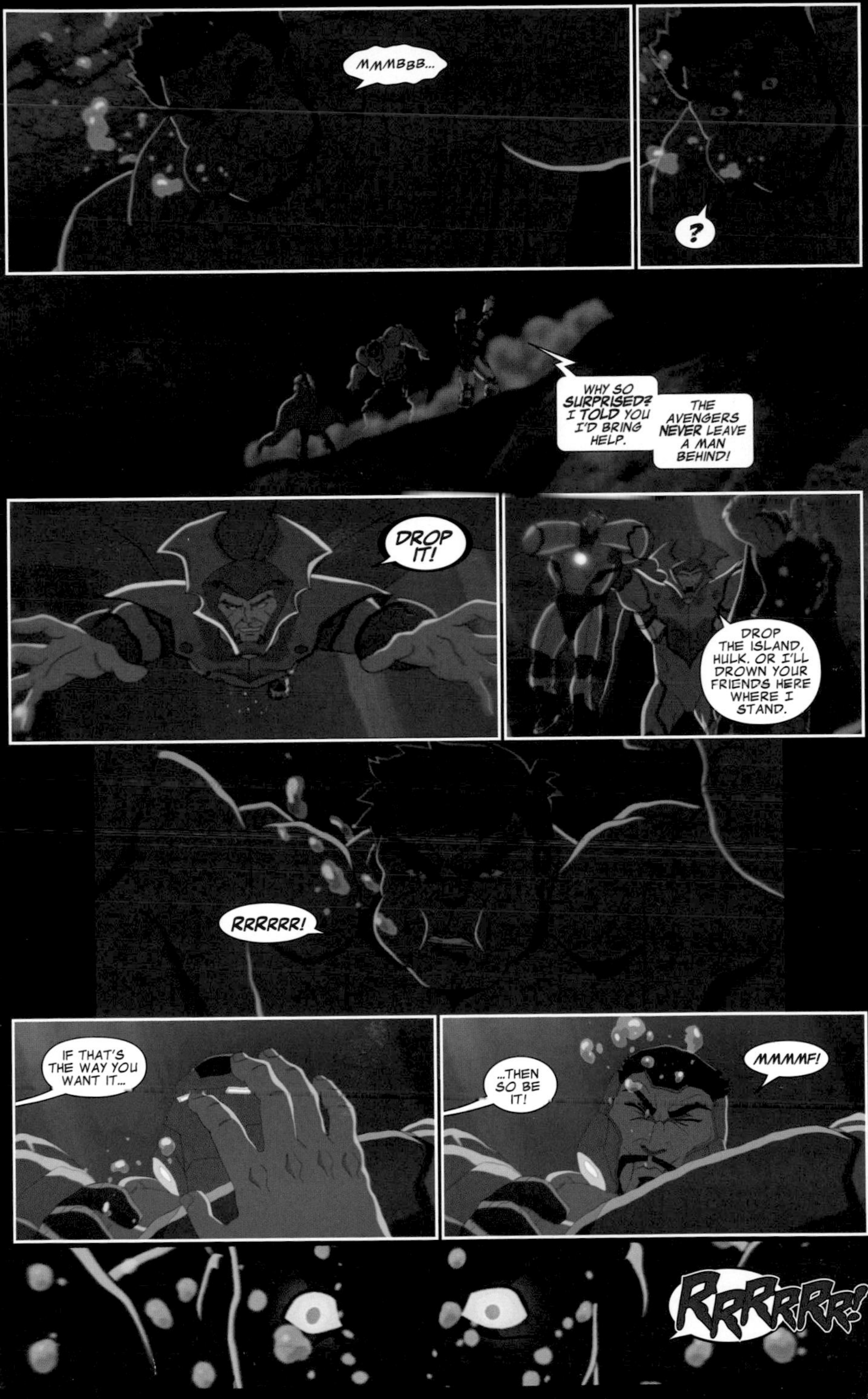
MMMBBB...
?
WHY SO SURPRISED? I TOLD YOU I'D BRING HELP.
THE AVENGERS NEVER LEAVE A MAN BEHIND!
DROP IT!
DROP THE ISLAND, HULK. OR I'LL DROWN YOUR FRIENDS HERE WHERE I STAND.
RRRRRR!
IF THAT'S THE WAY YOU WANT IT...
...THEN SO BE IT!
MMMMF!
RRRRRR!

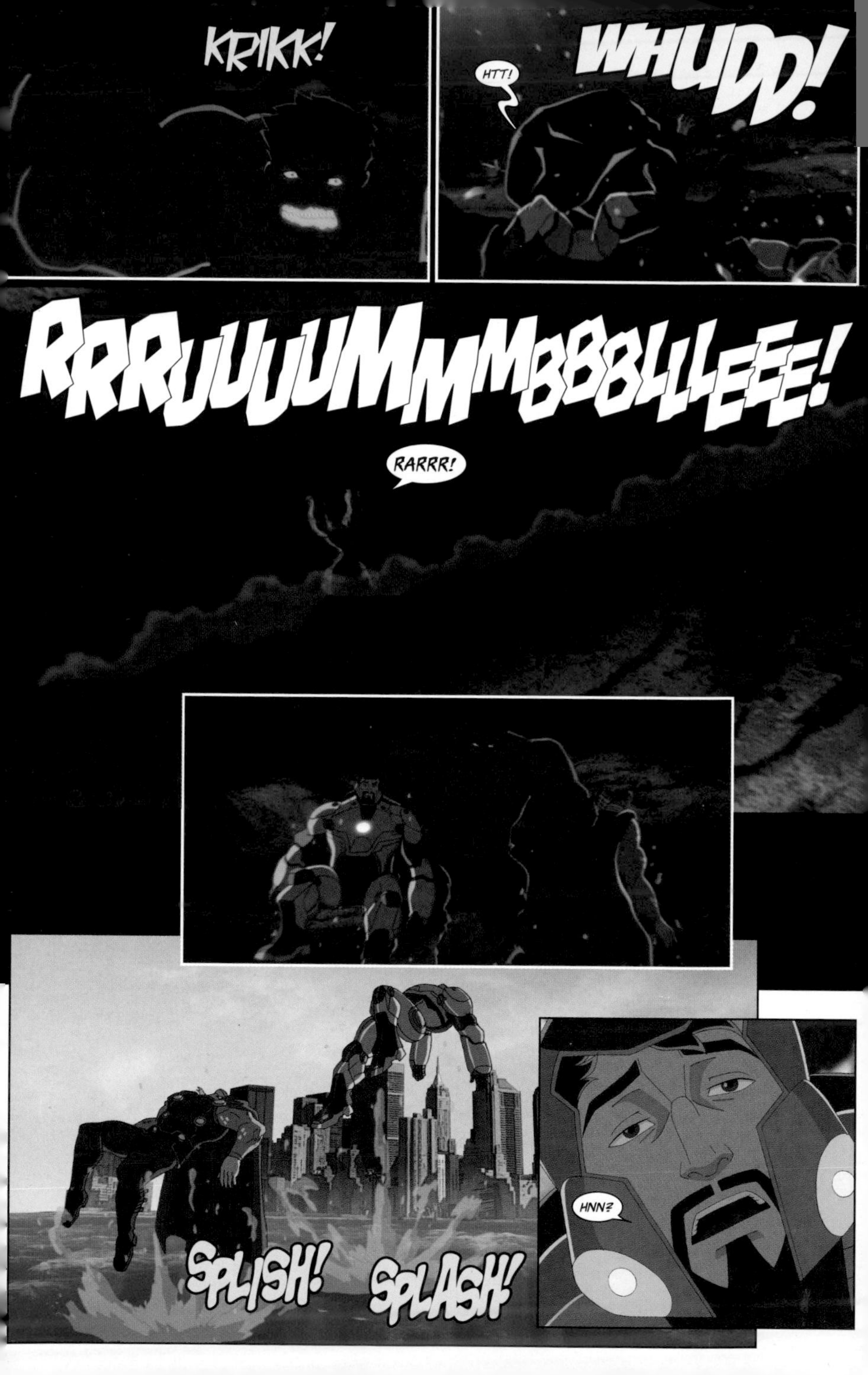
KRIKK!
HTT!
WHUDD!
RRRUUUUMMMBBBLLLEEE!
RARRR!
SPLISH!
SPLASH!
HNN?

NO NO NO! WE HAVE TO GET BACK DOWN THERE!

ATTUMA WAS TOO MUCH FOR HULK TO HANDLE ON LAND. HE'S EVEN MORE POWERFUL UNDER WATER--

SKRFFFH!!

NEVER MIND.

CRASH!

LIKE I SAID--NOBODY FLOODS MY CITY AND GETS AWAY WITH IT.

YOU THINK YOU'VE WON?

THIS IS FAR FROM--

RRRRRR!

RRROOAAARR!

CRUNCH!

NOW WE'VE WON.

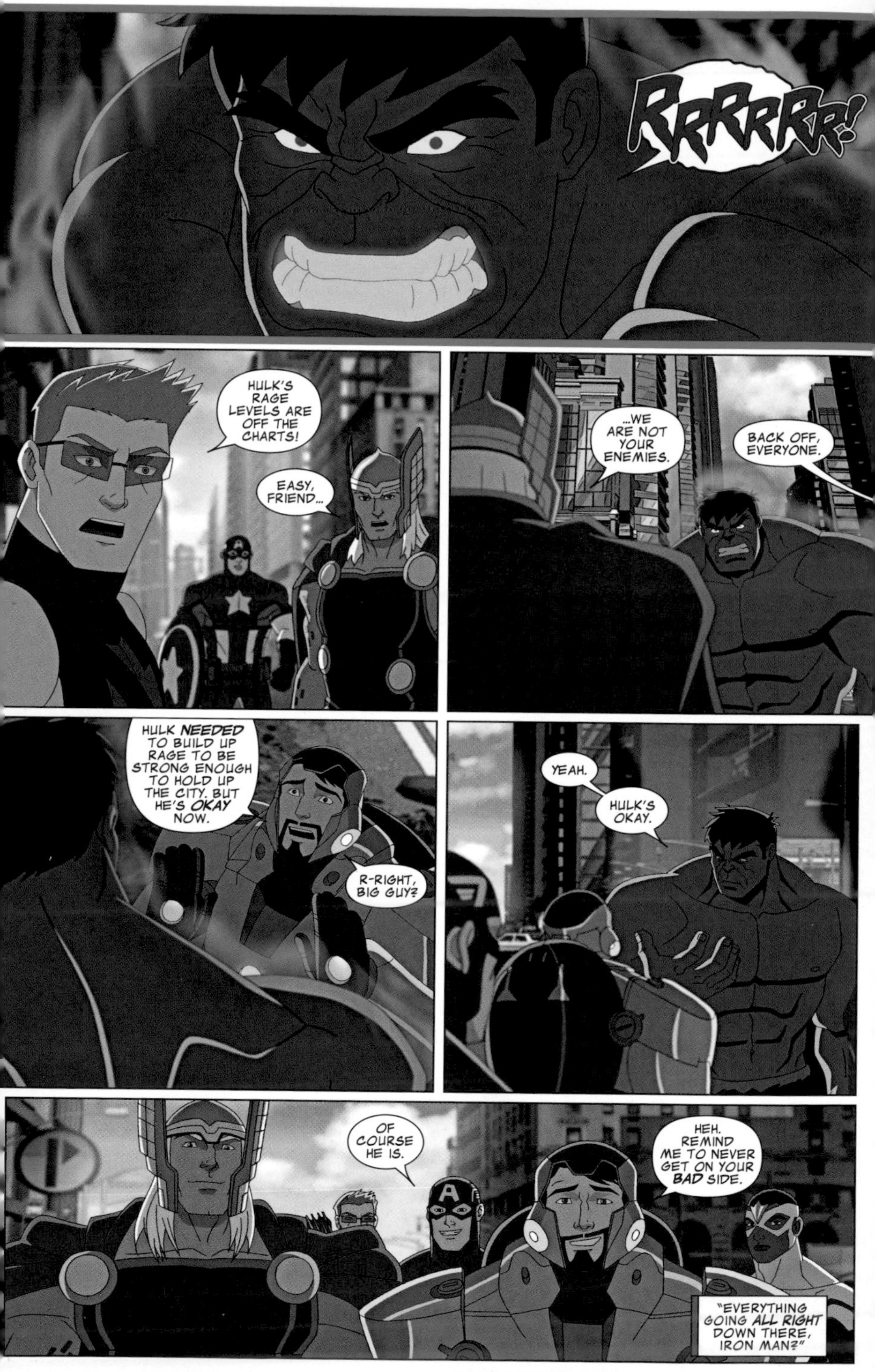
RRRRRR!
HULK'S RAGE LEVELS ARE OFF THE CHARTS!
EASY, FRIEND...
...WE ARE NOT YOUR ENEMIES.
BACK OFF, EVERYONE.
HULK NEEDED TO BUILD UP RAGE TO BE STRONG ENOUGH TO HOLD UP THE CITY. BUT HE'S OKAY NOW.
R-RIGHT, BIG GUY?
YEAH.
HULK'S OKAY.
OF COURSE HE IS.
HEH. REMIND ME TO NEVER GET ON YOUR BAD SIDE.
"EVERYTHING GOING ALL RIGHT DOWN THERE, IRON MAN?"

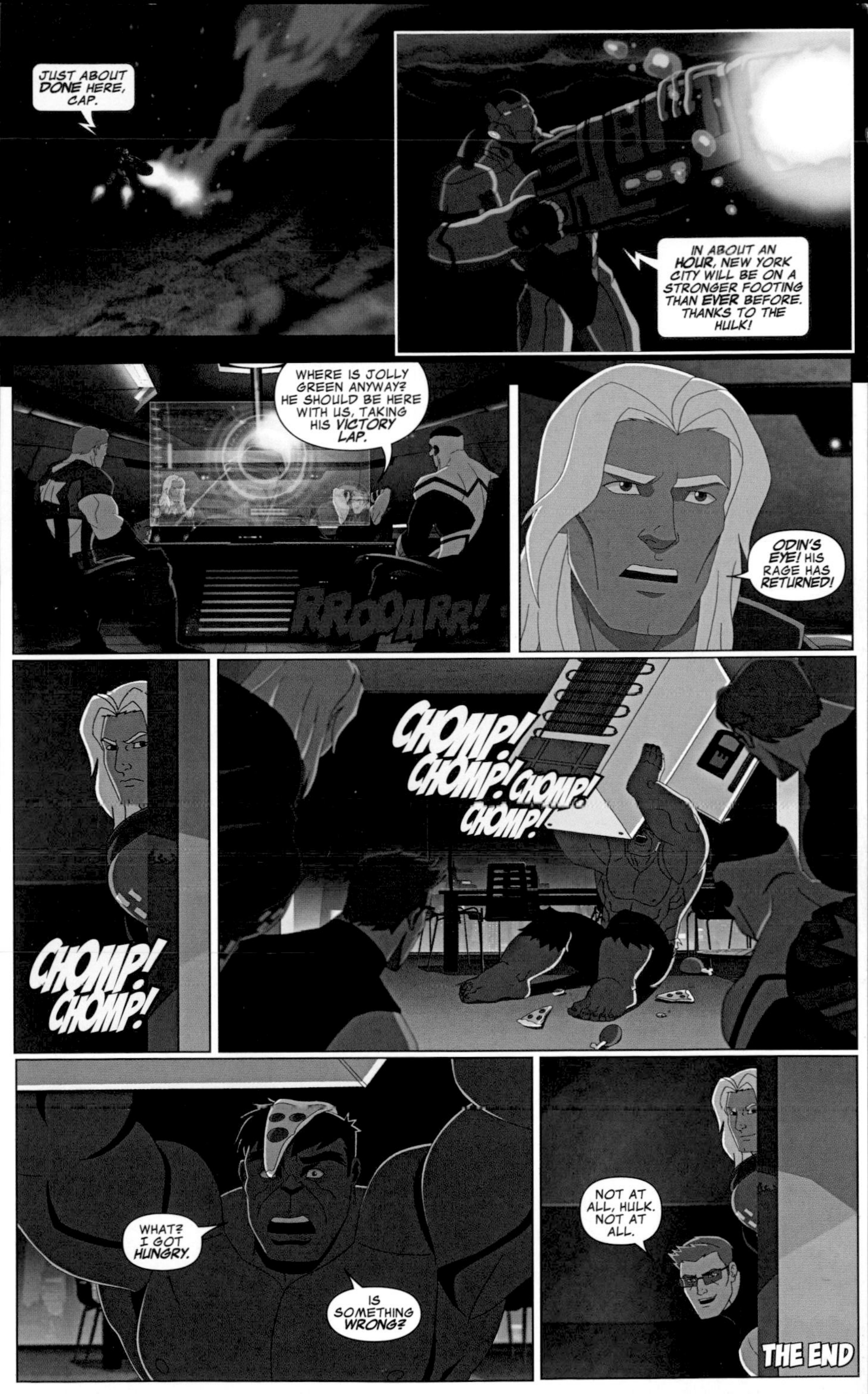
JUST ABOUT DONE HERE, CAP.
IN ABOUT AN HOUR, NEW YORK CITY WILL BE ON A STRONGER FOOTING THAN EVER BEFORE. THANKS TO THE HULK!
WHERE IS JOLLY GREEN ANYWAY? HE SHOULD BE HERE WITH US, TAKING HIS VICTORY LAP.
RRROOARR!
ODIN'S EYE! HIS RAGE HAS RETURNED!
CHOMP! CHOMP!
CHOMP! CHOMP! CHOMP! CHOMP!
WHAT? I GOT HUNGRY.
IS SOMETHING WRONG?
NOT AT ALL, HULK. NOT AT ALL.
THE END

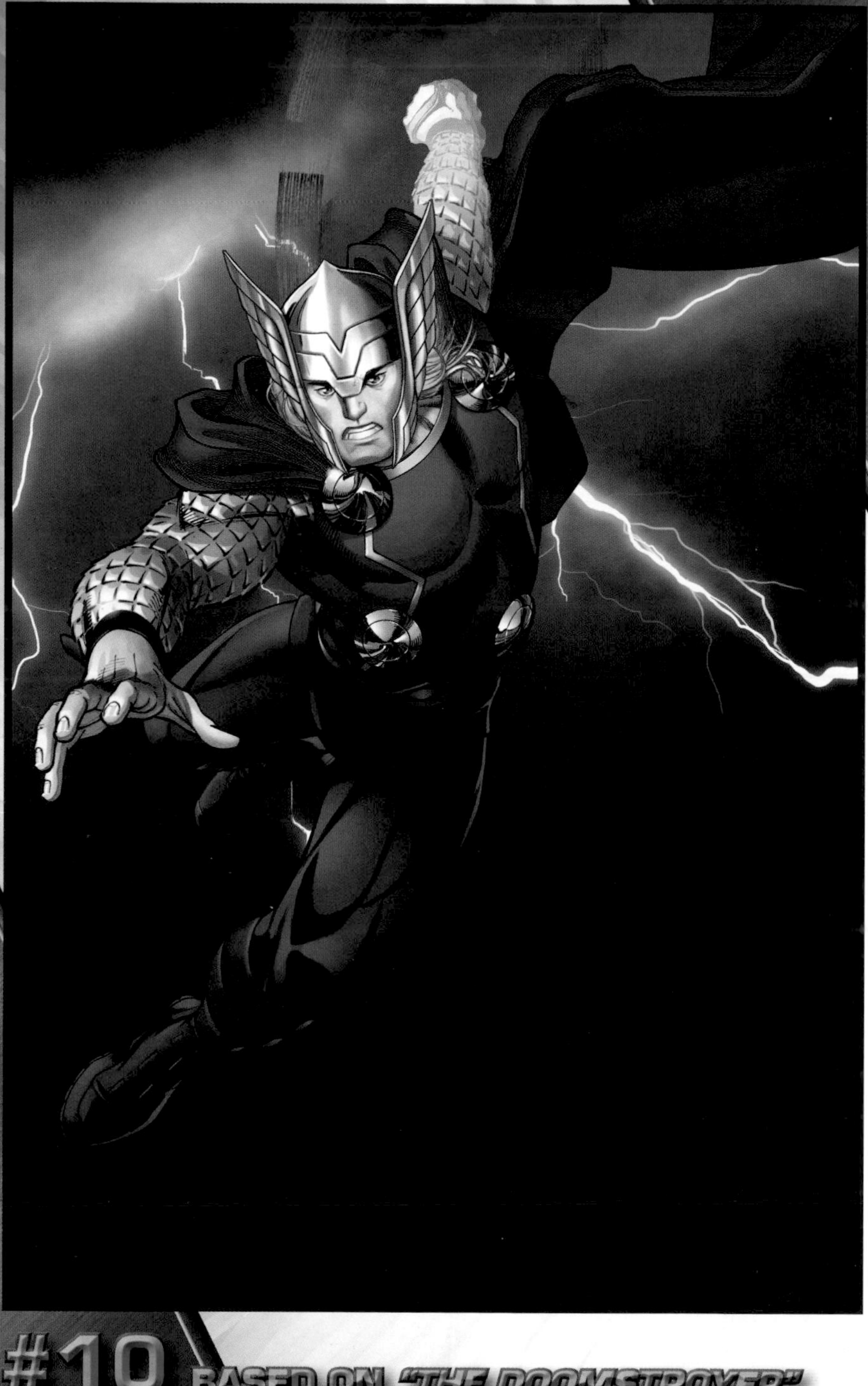

#10 BASED ON "THE DOOMSTROYER"

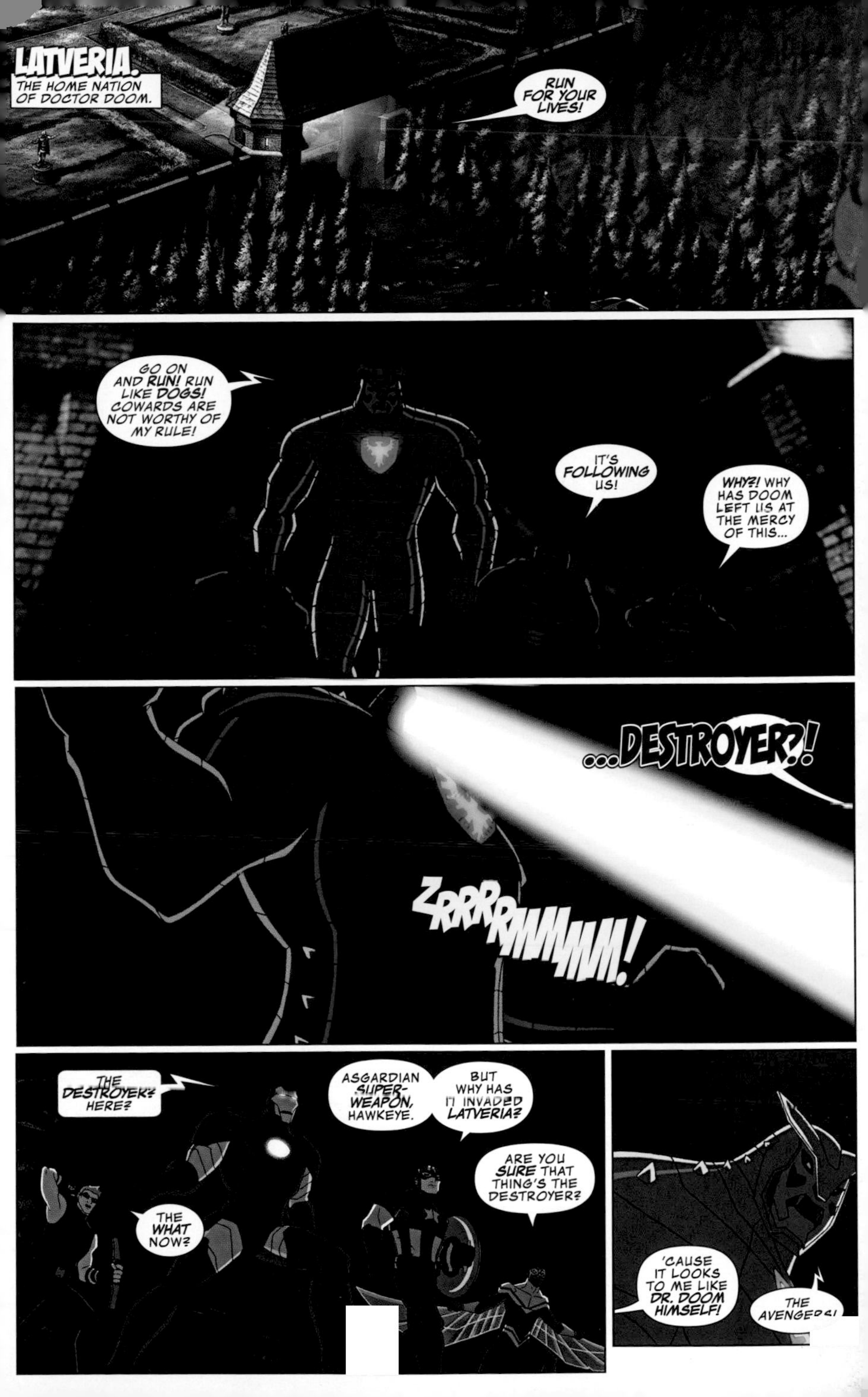
LATVERIA.
THE HOME NATION OF DOCTOR DOOM.
RUN FOR YOUR LIVES!
GO ON AND RUN! RUN LIKE DOGS! COWARDS ARE NOT WORTHY OF MY RULE!
IT'S FOLLOWING US!
WHY?! WHY HAS DOOM LEFT US AT THE MERCY OF THIS...
...DESTROYER?!
ZRRRRMMMMMM!
THE DESTROYER? HERE?
ASGARDIAN SUPER-WEAPON, HAWKEYE.
BUT WHY HAS IT INVADED LATVERIA?
THE WHAT NOW?
ARE YOU SURE THAT THING'S THE DESTROYER?
'CAUSE IT LOOKS TO ME LIKE DR. DOOM HIMSELF!

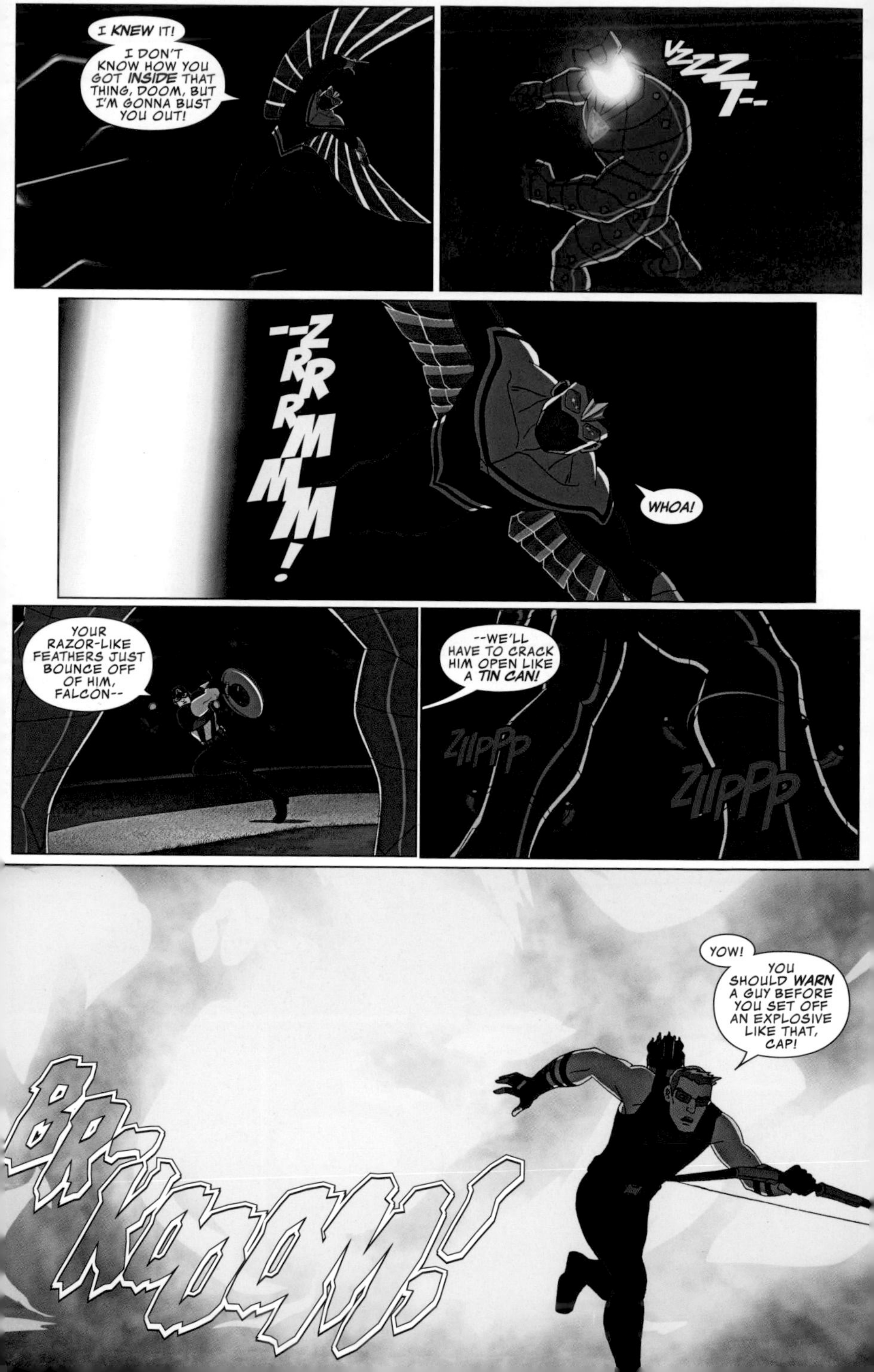
I KNEW IT!
I DON'T KNOW HOW YOU GOT INSIDE THAT THING, DOOM, BUT I'M GONNA BUST YOU OUT!
VZZZT--
--ZRRRMMMM!
WHOA!
YOUR RAZOR-LIKE FEATHERS JUST BOUNCE OFF OF HIM, FALCON--
--WE'LL HAVE TO CRACK HIM OPEN LIKE A TIN CAN!
ZIIPPP
ZIIPPP
BRKOOOM!
YOW!
YOU SHOULD WARN A GUY BEFORE YOU SET OFF AN EXPLOSIVE LIKE THAT, CAP!

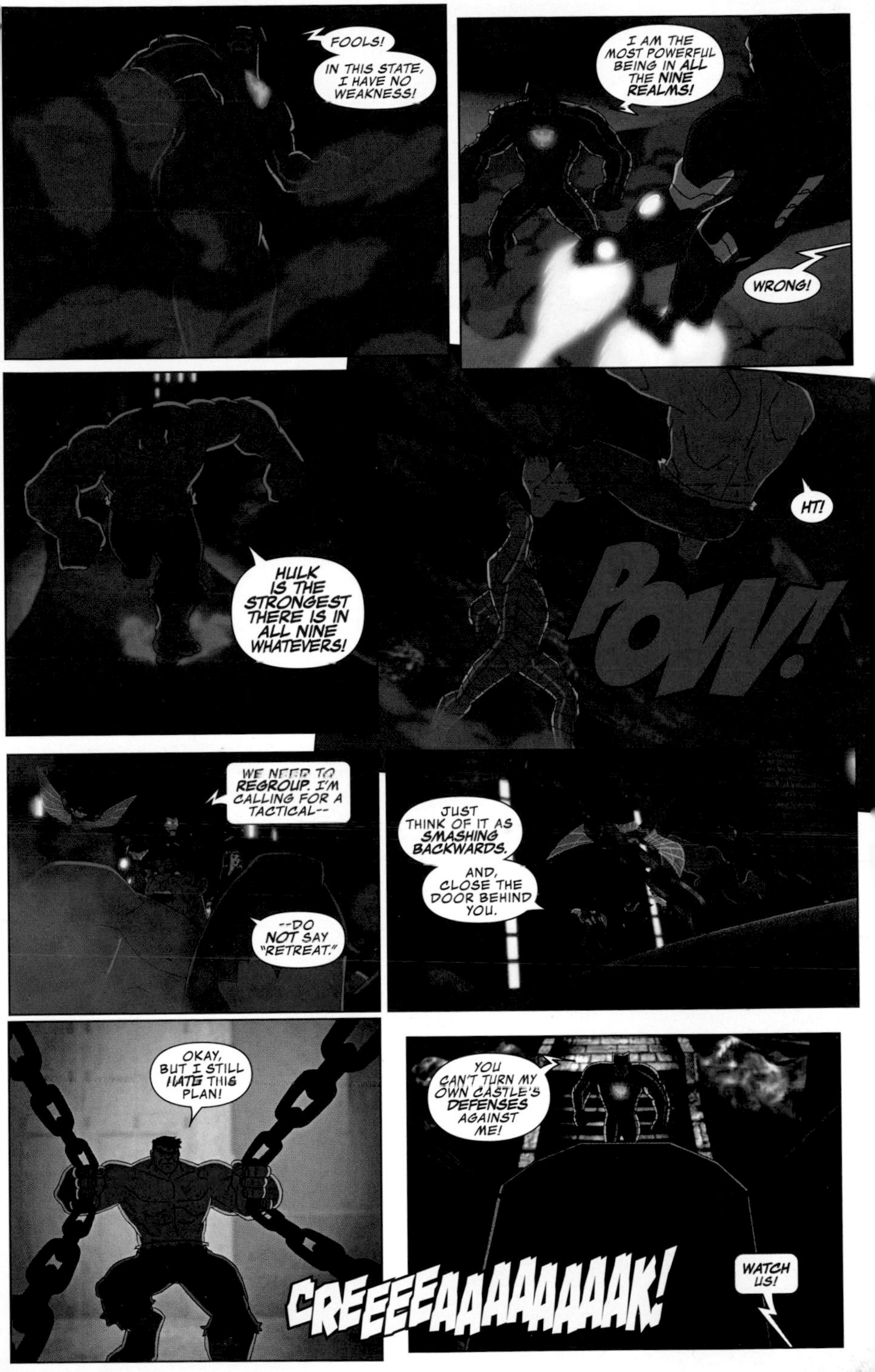

FOOLS!
IN THIS STATE, I HAVE NO WEAKNESS!
I AM THE MOST POWERFUL BEING IN ALL THE NINE REALMS!
WRONG!
HULK IS THE STRONGEST THERE IS IN ALL NINE WHATEVERS!
HT!
POW!
WE NEED TO REGROUP. I'M CALLING FOR A TACTICAL--
--DO NOT SAY "RETREAT."
JUST THINK OF IT AS SMASHING BACKWARDS.
AND, CLOSE THE DOOR BEHIND YOU.
OKAY, BUT I STILL HATE THIS PLAN!
CREEEEAAAAAAAK!
YOU CAN'T TURN MY OWN CASTLE'S DEFENSES AGAINST ME!
WATCH US!

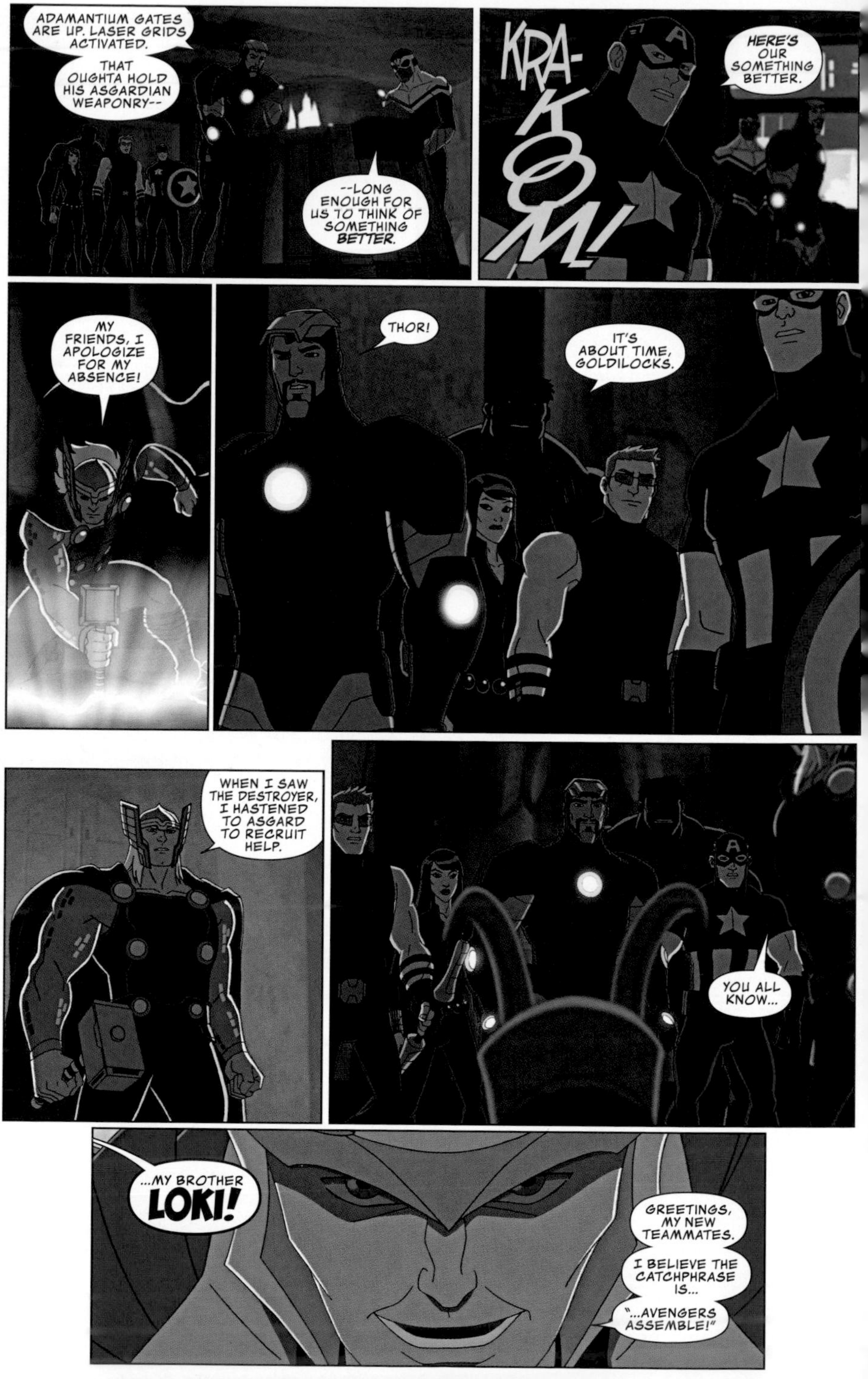
ADAMANTIUM GATES ARE UP. LASER GRIDS ACTIVATED.
THAT OUGHTA HOLD HIS ASGARDIAN WEAPONRY--
--LONG ENOUGH FOR US TO THINK OF SOMETHING BETTER.
KRA-KOOM!
HERE'S OUR SOMETHING BETTER.
MY FRIENDS, I APOLOGIZE FOR MY ABSENCE!
THOR!
IT'S ABOUT TIME, GOLDILOCKS.
WHEN I SAW THE DESTROYER, I HASTENED TO ASGARD TO RECRUIT HELP.
YOU ALL KNOW...
...MY BROTHER LOKI!
GREETINGS, MY NEW TEAMMATES.
I BELIEVE THE CATCHPHRASE IS...
"...AVENGERS ASSEMBLE!"

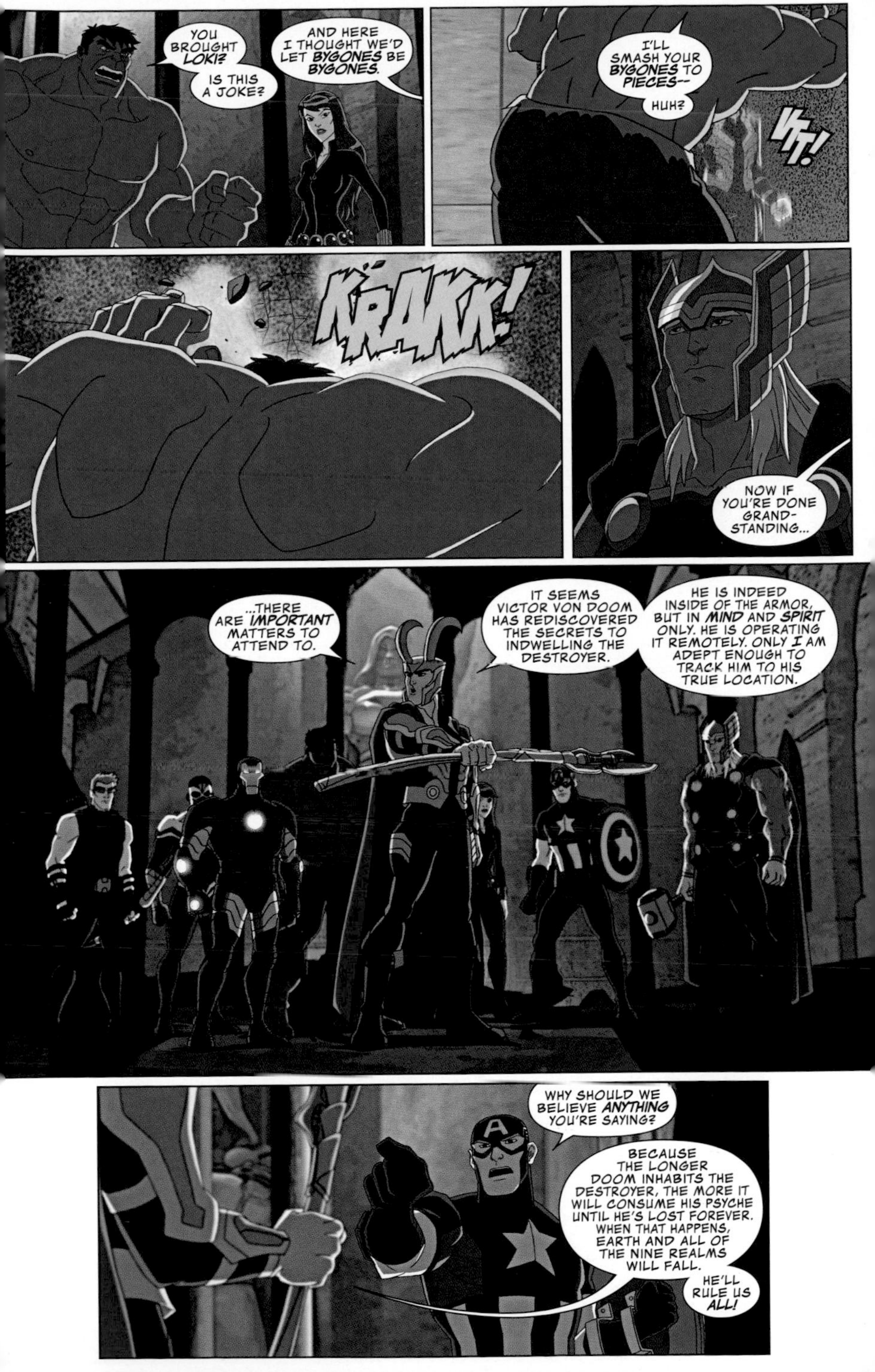
YOU BROUGHT LOKI?
IS THIS A JOKE?
AND HERE I THOUGHT WE'D LET BYGONES BE BYGONES.
I'LL SMASH YOUR BYGONES TO PIECES--
HUH?
KT!
KRAKK!
NOW IF YOU'RE DONE GRAND-STANDING...
...THERE ARE IMPORTANT MATTERS TO ATTEND TO.
IT SEEMS VICTOR VON DOOM HAS REDISCOVERED THE SECRETS TO INDWELLING THE DESTROYER.
HE IS INDEED INSIDE OF THE ARMOR, BUT IN MIND AND SPIRIT ONLY. HE IS OPERATING IT REMOTELY. ONLY I AM ADEPT ENOUGH TO TRACK HIM TO HIS TRUE LOCATION.
WHY SHOULD WE BELIEVE ANYTHING YOU'RE SAYING?
BECAUSE THE LONGER DOOM INHABITS THE DESTROYER, THE MORE IT WILL CONSUME HIS PSYCHE UNTIL HE'S LOST FOREVER. WHEN THAT HAPPENS, EARTH AND ALL OF THE NINE REALMS WILL FALL.
HE'LL RULE US ALL!

BRKOOM!

SCHLIK

DOOM-STROYER'S COMING! WE MUST HURRY!

BWOM!

THIS PORTAL WILL TAKE US TO HIM.

OKAY, TWO TEAMS--

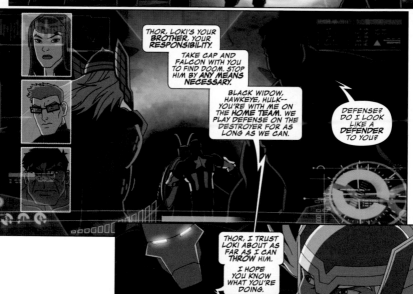

THOR, LOKI'S YOUR **BROTHER.** YOUR **RESPONSIBILITY.**

TAKE CAP AND FALCON WITH YOU TO FIND DOOM. STOP HIM BY *ANY MEANS* NECESSARY.

BLACK WIDOW, HAWKEYE, HULK-- YOU'RE WITH ME ON THE **HOME TEAM.** WE PLAY DEFENSE ON THE DESTROYER FOR AS LONG AS WE CAN.

DEFENSE? DO I LOOK LIKE A **DEFENDER** TO YOU?

THOR, I TRUST LOKI ABOUT AS FAR AS I CAN THROW HIM.

I HOPE YOU KNOW WHAT YOU'RE DOING.

IF HE BETRAYS US...

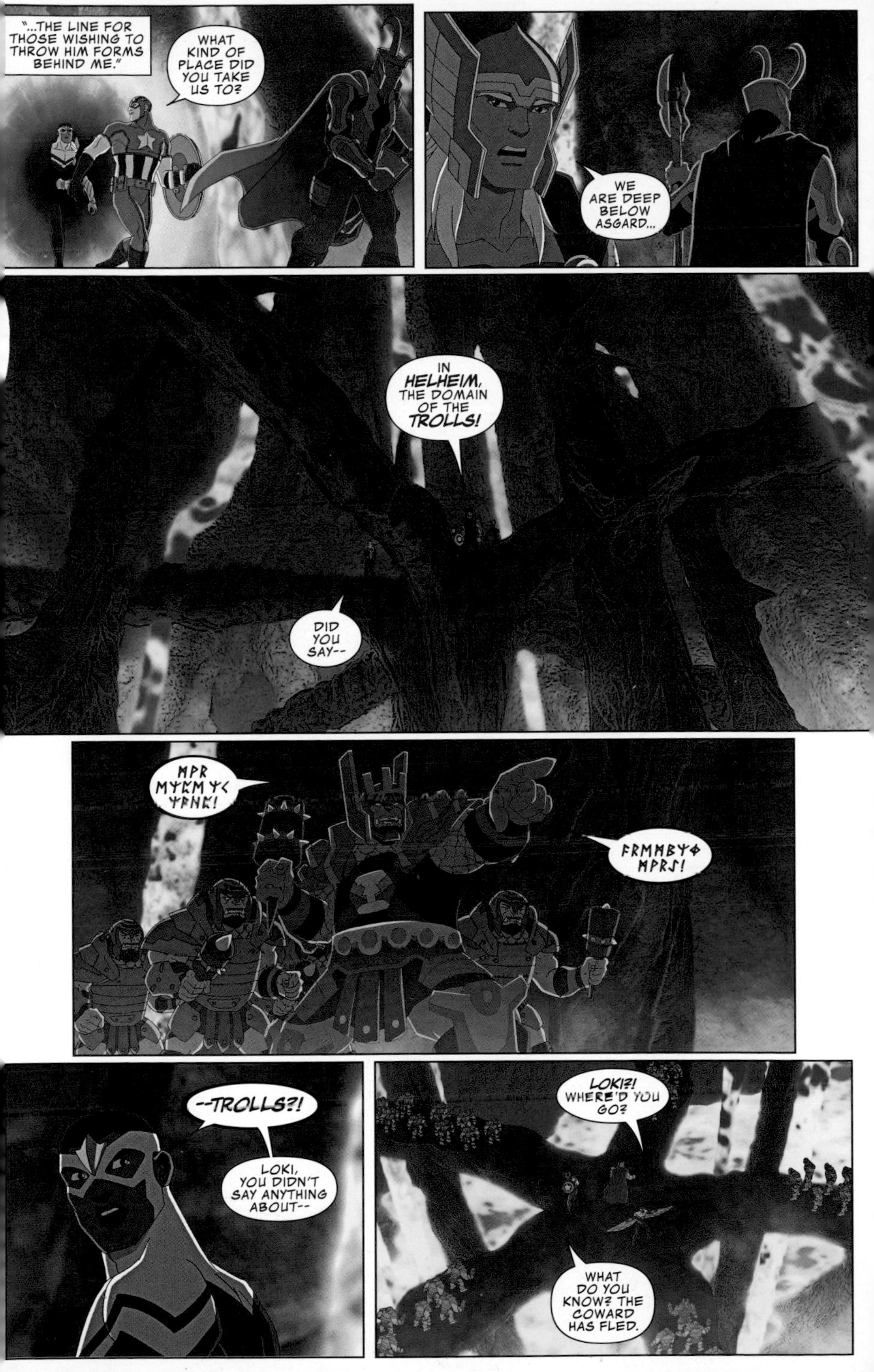
"...THE LINE FOR THOSE WISHING TO THROW HIM FORMS BEHIND ME."
WHAT KIND OF PLACE DID YOU TAKE US TO?
WE ARE DEEP BELOW ASGARD...
IN HELHEIM, THE DOMAIN OF THE TROLLS!
DID YOU SAY--
--TROLLS?!
LOKI, YOU DIDN'T SAY ANYTHING ABOUT--
LOKI?! WHERE'D YOU GO?
WHAT DO YOU KNOW? THE COWARD HAS FLED.

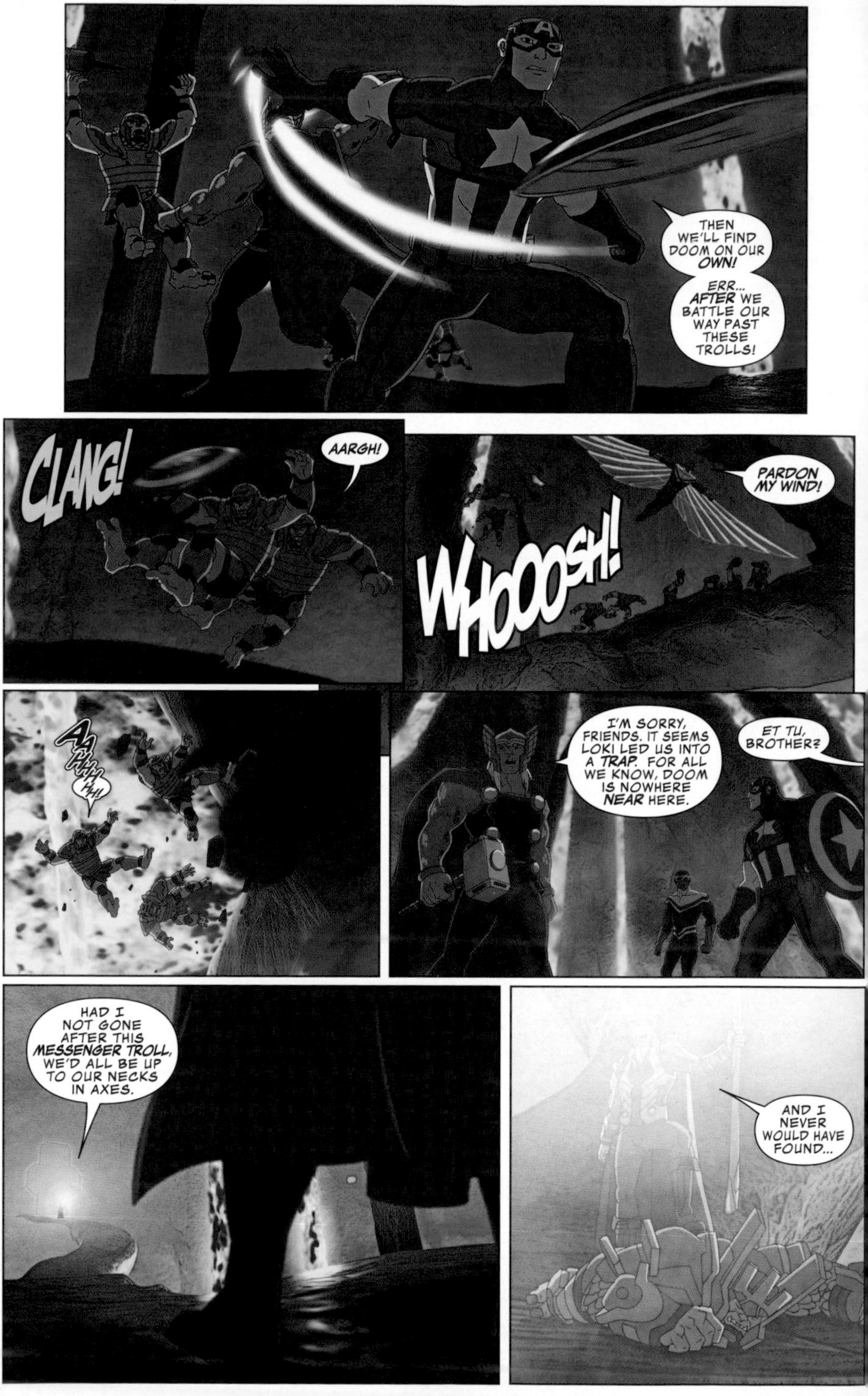
THEN WE'LL FIND DOOM ON OUR OWN!
ERR... AFTER WE BATTLE OUR WAY PAST THESE TROLLS!
CLANG!
AARGH!
PARDON MY WIND!
WHOOOSH!
AAHHHHH!
I'M SORRY, FRIENDS. IT SEEMS LOKI LED US INTO A TRAP. FOR ALL WE KNOW, DOOM IS NOWHERE NEAR HERE.
ET TU, BROTHER?
HAD I NOT GONE AFTER THIS MESSENGER TROLL, WE'D ALL BE UP TO OUR NECKS IN AXES.
AND I NEVER WOULD HAVE FOUND...

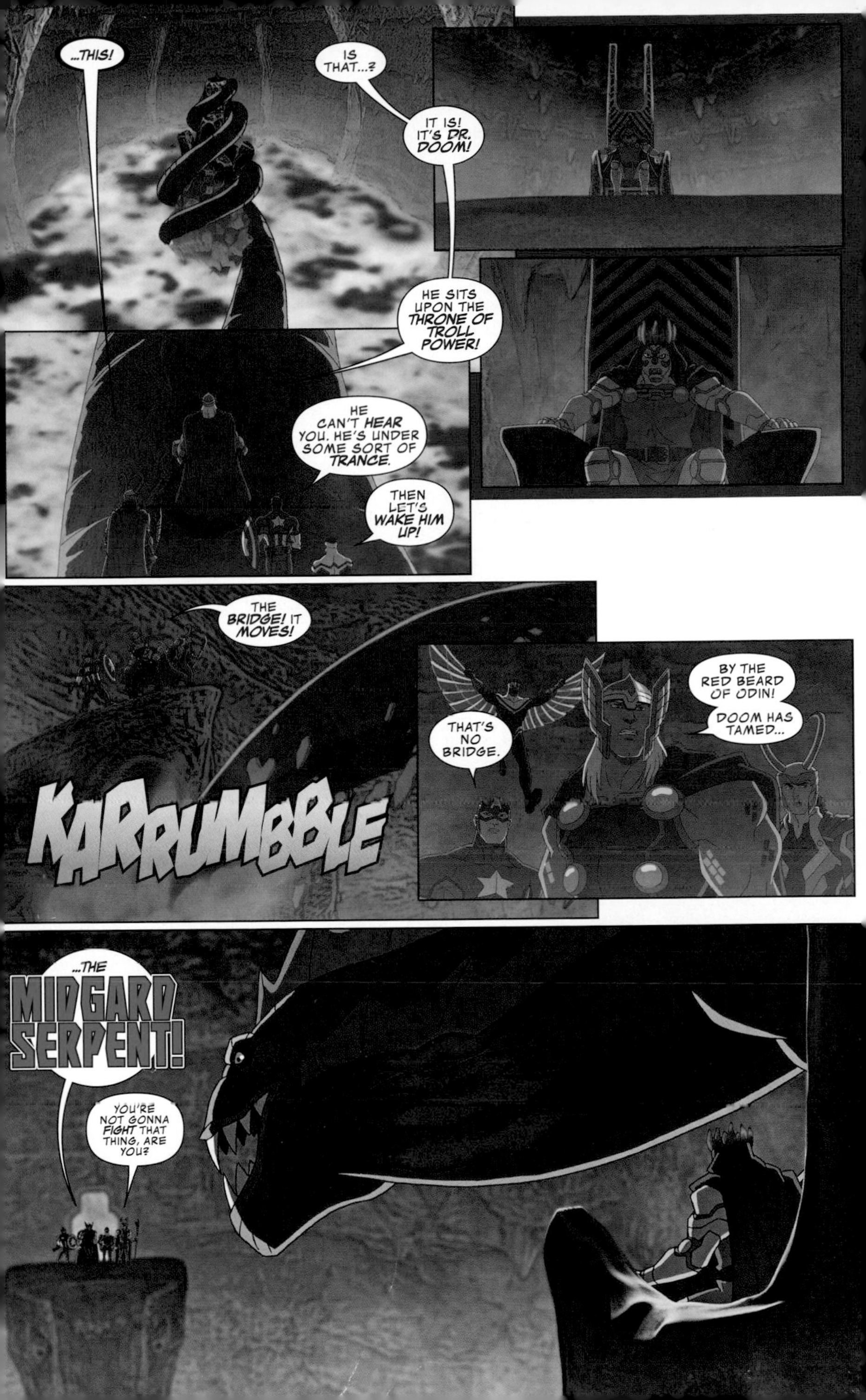
...THIS!
IS THAT...?
IT IS! IT'S DR. DOOM!
HE SITS UPON THE THRONE OF TROLL POWER!
HE CAN'T HEAR YOU. HE'S UNDER SOME SORT OF TRANCE.
THEN LET'S WAKE HIM UP!
THE BRIDGE! IT MOVES!
KARRUMBBLE
THAT'S NO BRIDGE.
BY THE RED BEARD OF ODIN!
DOOM HAS TAMED...
...THE MIDGARD SERPENT!
YOU'RE NOT GONNA FIGHT THAT THING, ARE YOU?

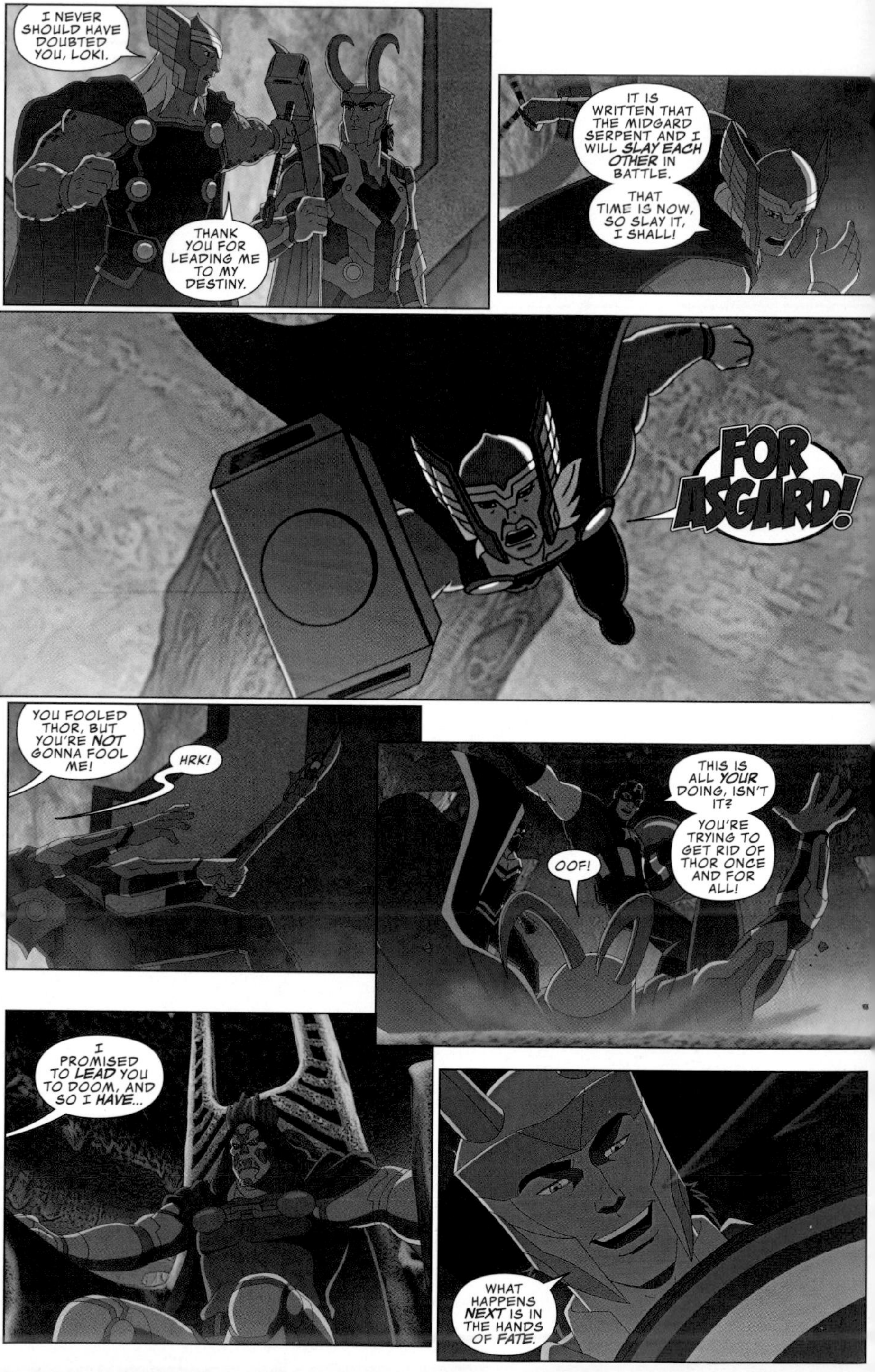
I NEVER SHOULD HAVE DOUBTED YOU, LOKI.
THANK YOU FOR LEADING ME TO MY DESTINY.
IT IS WRITTEN THAT THE MIDGARD SERPENT AND I WILL SLAY EACH OTHER IN BATTLE.
THAT TIME IS NOW, SO SLAY IT, I SHALL!
FOR ASGARD!
YOU FOOLED THOR, BUT YOU'RE NOT GONNA FOOL ME!
HRK!
THIS IS ALL YOUR DOING, ISN'T IT?
YOU'RE TRYING TO GET RID OF THOR ONCE AND FOR ALL!
OOF!
I PROMISED TO LEAD YOU TO DOOM, AND SO I HAVE...
WHAT HAPPENS NEXT IS IN THE HANDS OF FATE.

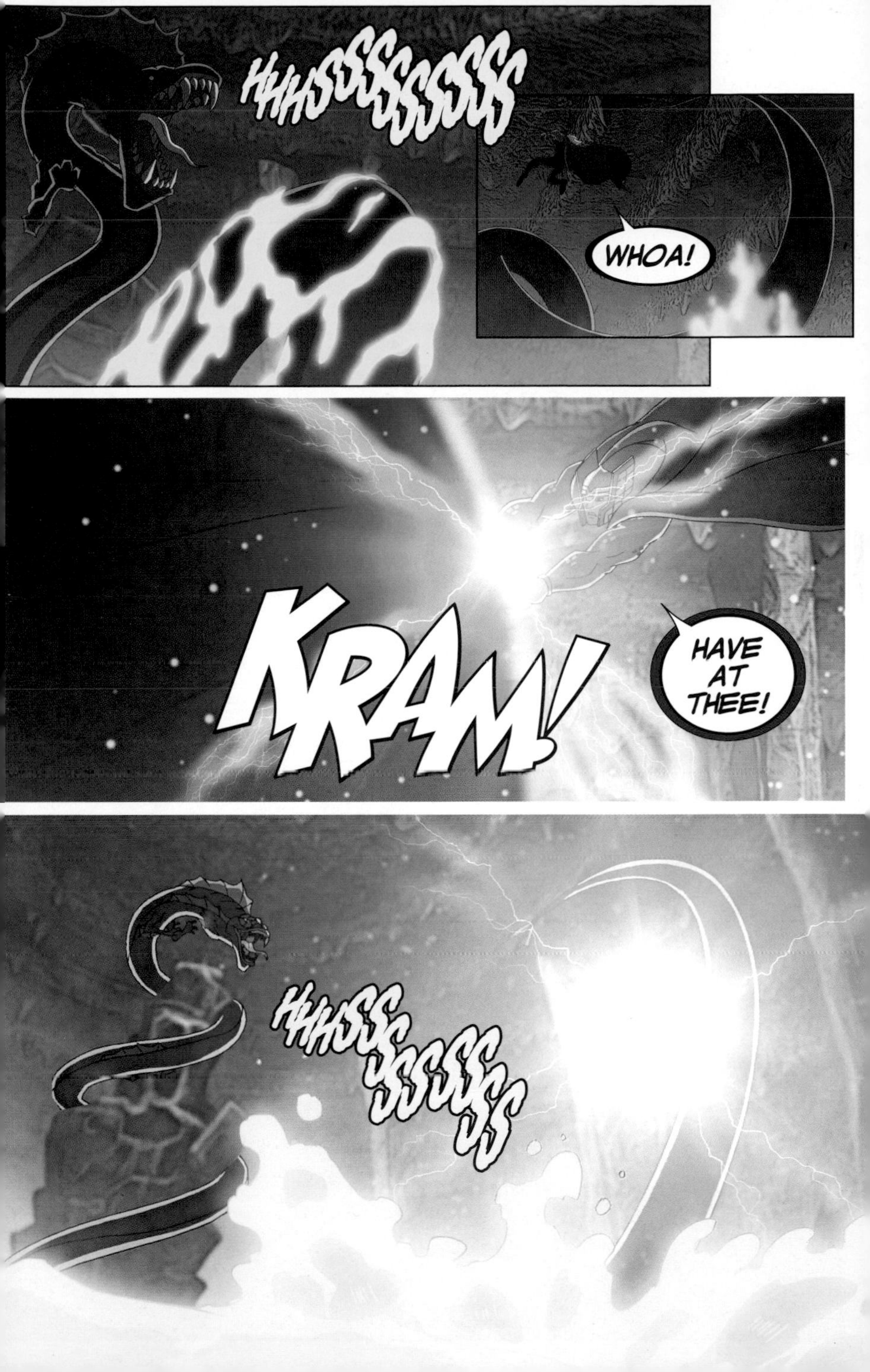
HHHSSSSSSSSSS
WHOA!
KRAM!
HAVE AT THEE!
HHHSSSSSSSSSS

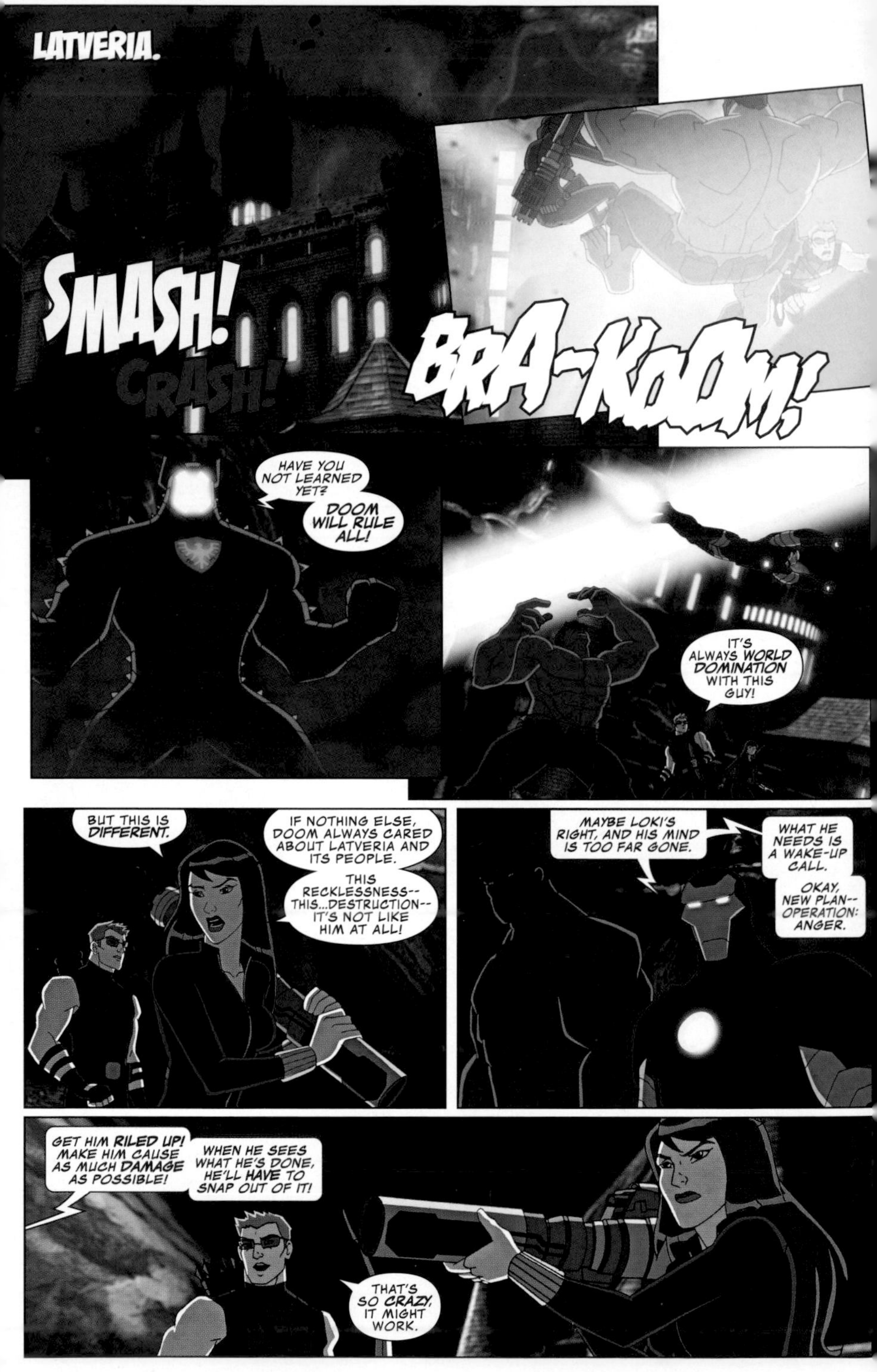
LATVERIA.
SMASH!
CRASH!
BRA-KOOM!
HAVE YOU NOT LEARNED YET? DOOM WILL RULE ALL!
IT'S ALWAYS WORLD DOMINATION WITH THIS GUY!
BUT THIS IS DIFFERENT.
IF NOTHING ELSE, DOOM ALWAYS CARED ABOUT LATVERIA AND ITS PEOPLE.
THIS RECKLESSNESS-- THIS...DESTRUCTION-- IT'S NOT LIKE HIM AT ALL!
MAYBE LOKI'S RIGHT, AND HIS MIND IS TOO FAR GONE.
WHAT HE NEEDS IS A WAKE-UP CALL.
OKAY, NEW PLAN-- OPERATION: ANGER.
GET HIM RILED UP! MAKE HIM CAUSE AS MUCH DAMAGE AS POSSIBLE!
WHEN HE SEES WHAT HE'S DONE, HE'LL HAVE TO SNAP OUT OF IT!
THAT'S SO CRAZY, IT MIGHT WORK.

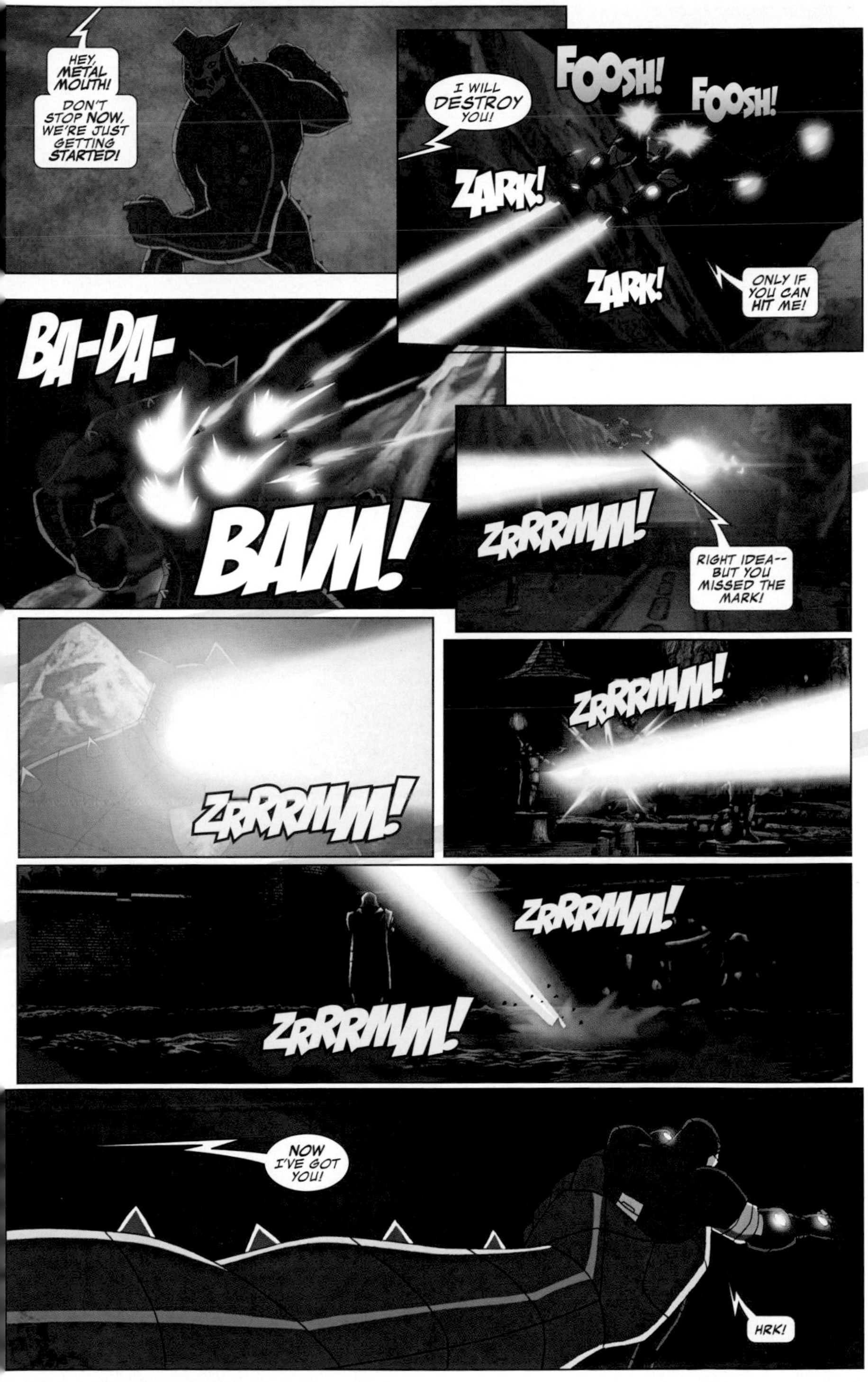
HEY, METAL MOUTH!
DON'T STOP NOW, WE'RE JUST GETTING STARTED!
I WILL DESTROY YOU!
FOOSH!
FOOSH!
ZARK!
ZARK!
ONLY IF YOU CAN HIT ME!
BA-DA-
BAM!
ZRRRMMM!
RIGHT IDEA-- BUT YOU MISSED THE MARK!
ZRRRMMM!
ZRRRMMM!
ZRRRMMM!
ZRRRMMM!
NOW I'VE GOT YOU!
HRK!

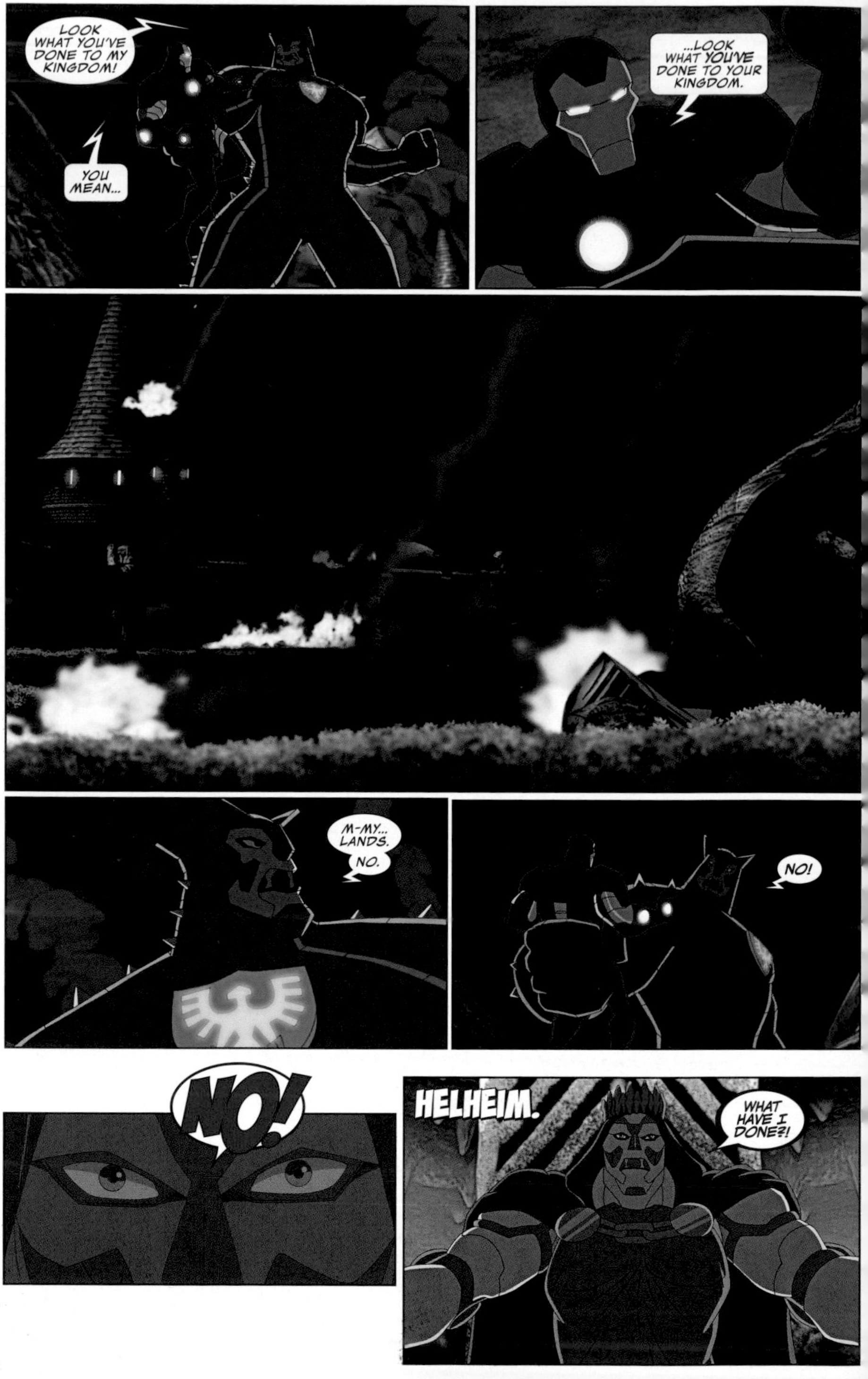
LOOK WHAT YOU'VE DONE TO MY KINGDOM!
YOU MEAN...
...LOOK WHAT YOU'VE DONE TO YOUR KINGDOM.
M-MY... LANDS.
NO.
NO!
NO!
HELHEIM.
WHAT HAVE I DONE?!

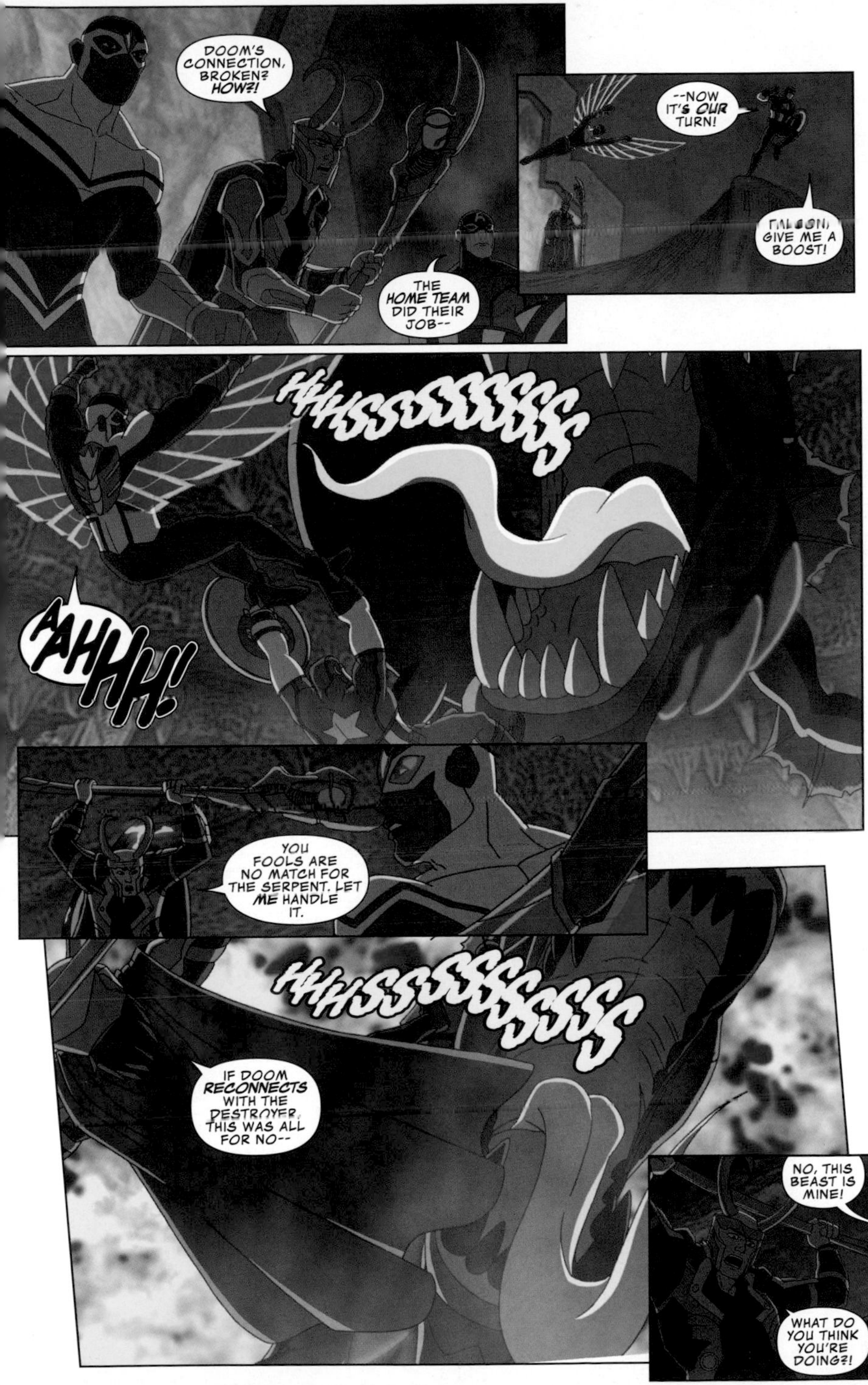
DOOM'S CONNECTION, BROKEN?! HOW?!
THE HOME TEAM DID THEIR JOB--
--NOW IT'S OUR TURN!
GIVE ME A BOOST!
HHHSSSSSSSSS
AAHHH!
YOU FOOLS ARE NO MATCH FOR THE SERPENT. LET ME HANDLE IT.
HHHSSSSSSSSSSS
IF DOOM RECONNECTS WITH THE DESTROYER, THIS WAS ALL FOR NO--
NO, THIS BEAST IS MINE!
WHAT DO YOU THINK YOU'RE DOING?!

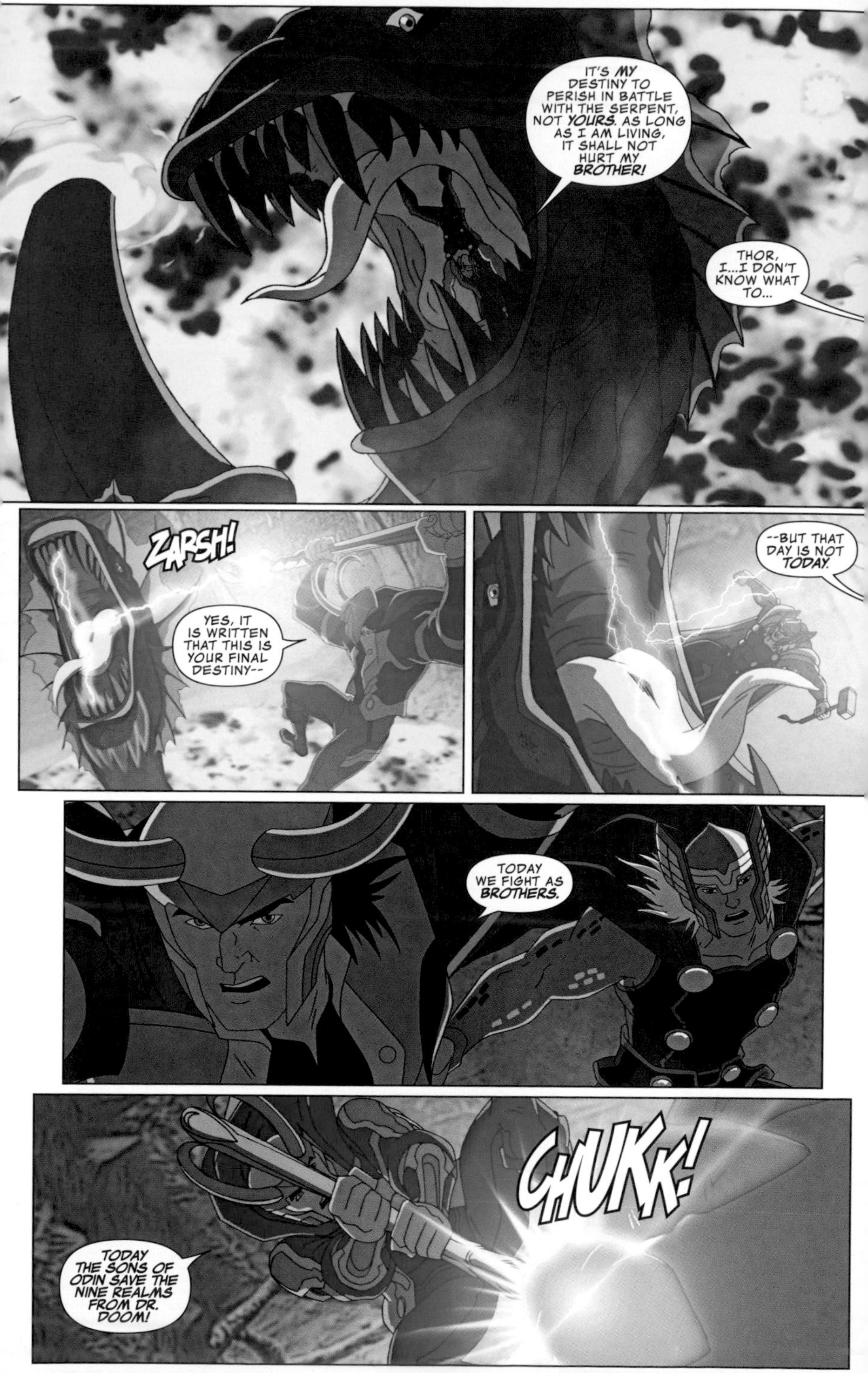

IT'S MY DESTINY TO PERISH IN BATTLE WITH THE SERPENT, NOT YOURS. AS LONG AS I AM LIVING, IT SHALL NOT HURT MY BROTHER!
THOR, I...I DON'T KNOW WHAT TO...
ZARSH!
YES, IT IS WRITTEN THAT THIS IS YOUR FINAL DESTINY--
--BUT THAT DAY IS NOT TODAY.
TODAY WE FIGHT AS BROTHERS.
CHUKK!
TODAY THE SONS OF ODIN SAVE THE NINE REALMS FROM DR. DOOM!

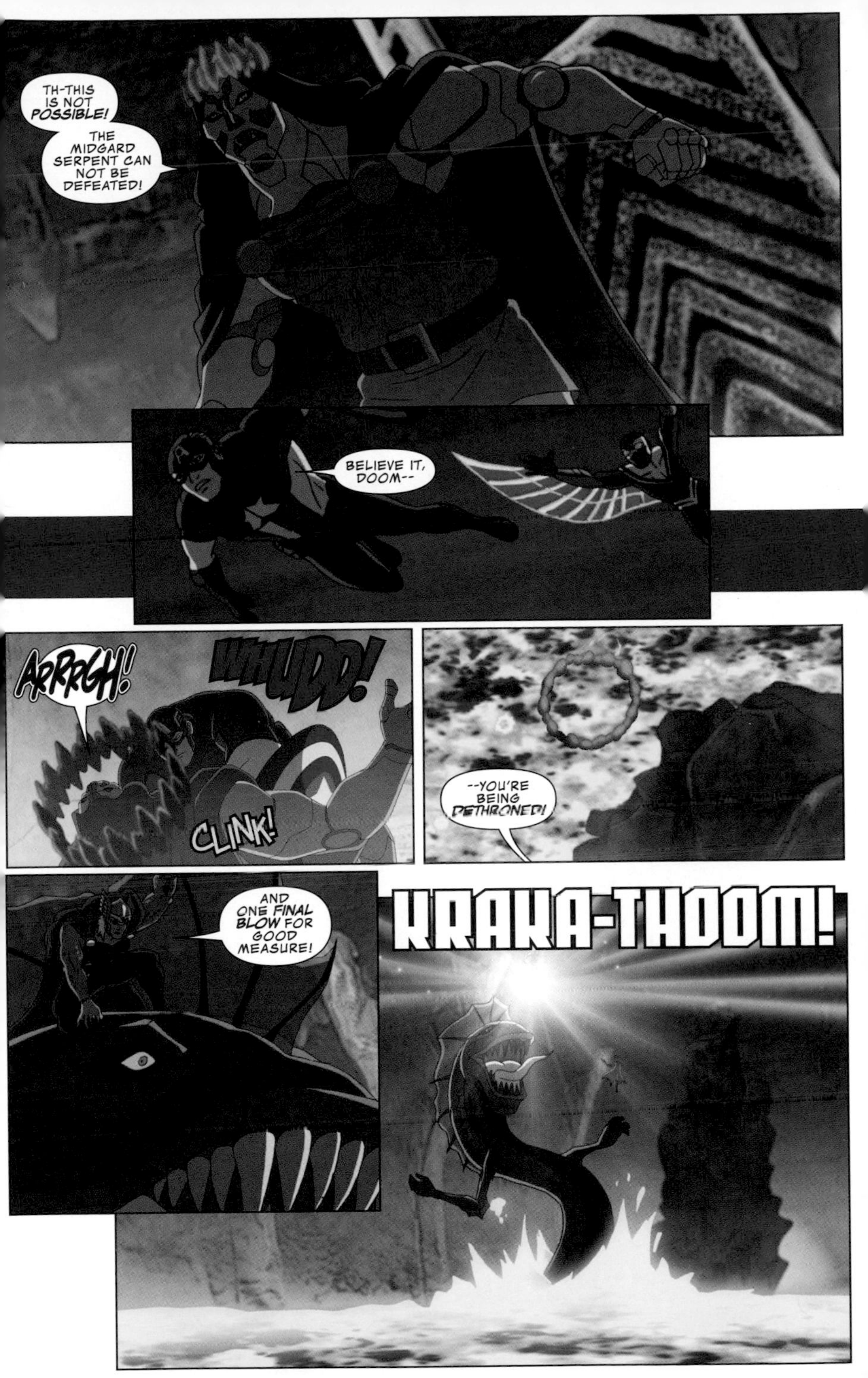
TH-THIS IS NOT POSSIBLE!
THE MIDGARD SERPENT CAN NOT BE DEFEATED!
BELIEVE IT, DOOM--
ARRRGH!
WHUDD!
CLINK!
--YOU'RE BEING DETHRONED!
AND ONE FINAL BLOW FOR GOOD MEASURE!
KRAKA-THOOM!

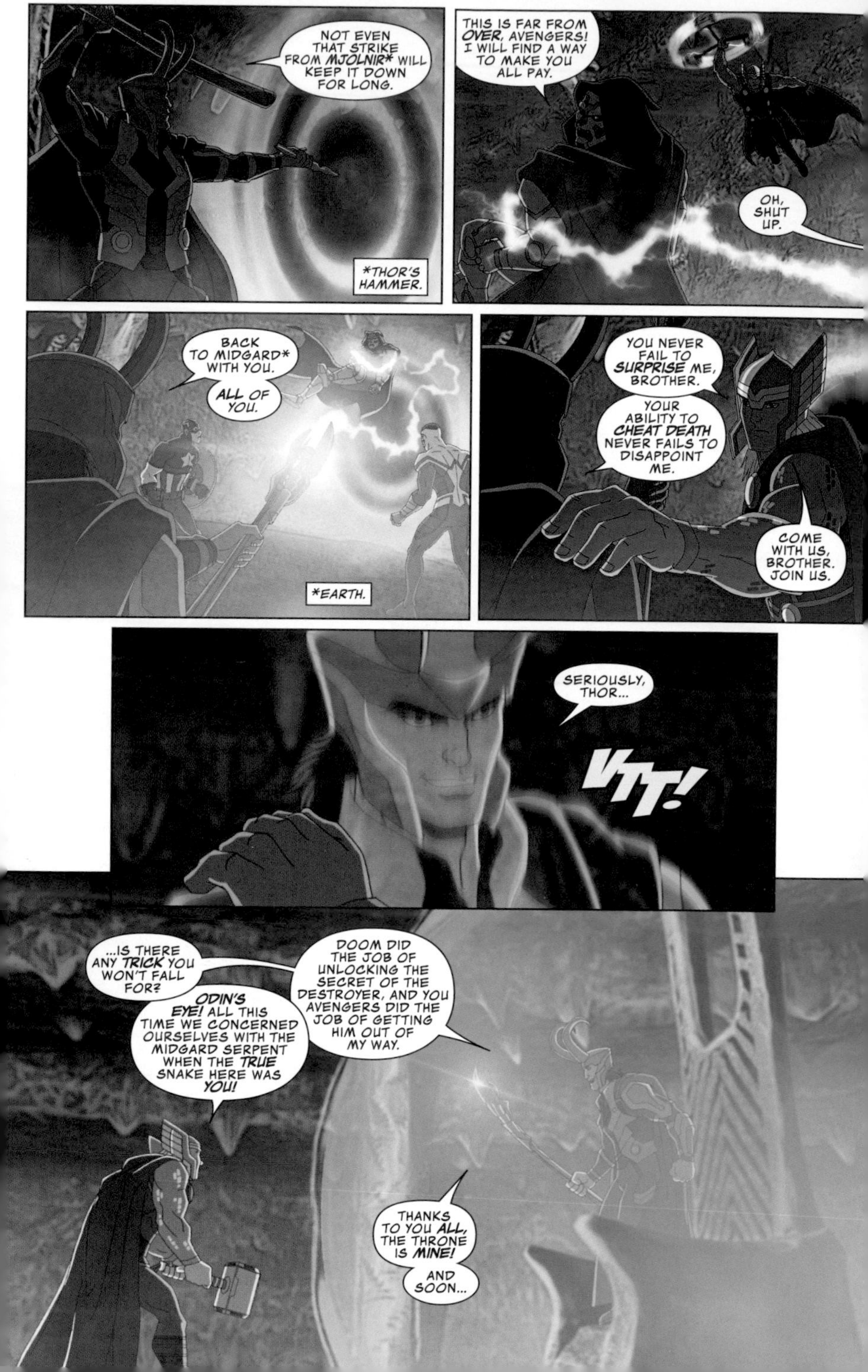
NOT EVEN THAT STRIKE FROM MJOLNIR* WILL KEEP IT DOWN FOR LONG.
*THOR'S HAMMER.
THIS IS FAR FROM OVER, AVENGERS! I WILL FIND A WAY TO MAKE YOU ALL PAY.
OH, SHUT UP.
BACK TO MIDGARD* WITH YOU.
ALL OF YOU.
*EARTH.
YOU NEVER FAIL TO SURPRISE ME, BROTHER.
YOUR ABILITY TO CHEAT DEATH NEVER FAILS TO DISAPPOINT ME.
COME WITH US, BROTHER. JOIN US.
SERIOUSLY, THOR...
VTT!
...IS THERE ANY TRICK YOU WON'T FALL FOR?
ODIN'S EYE! ALL THIS TIME WE CONCERNED OURSELVES WITH THE MIDGARD SERPENT WHEN THE TRUE SNAKE HERE WAS YOU!
DOOM DID THE JOB OF UNLOCKING THE SECRET OF THE DESTROYER, AND YOU AVENGERS DID THE JOB OF GETTING HIM OUT OF MY WAY.
THANKS TO YOU ALL, THE THRONE IS MINE!
AND SOON...

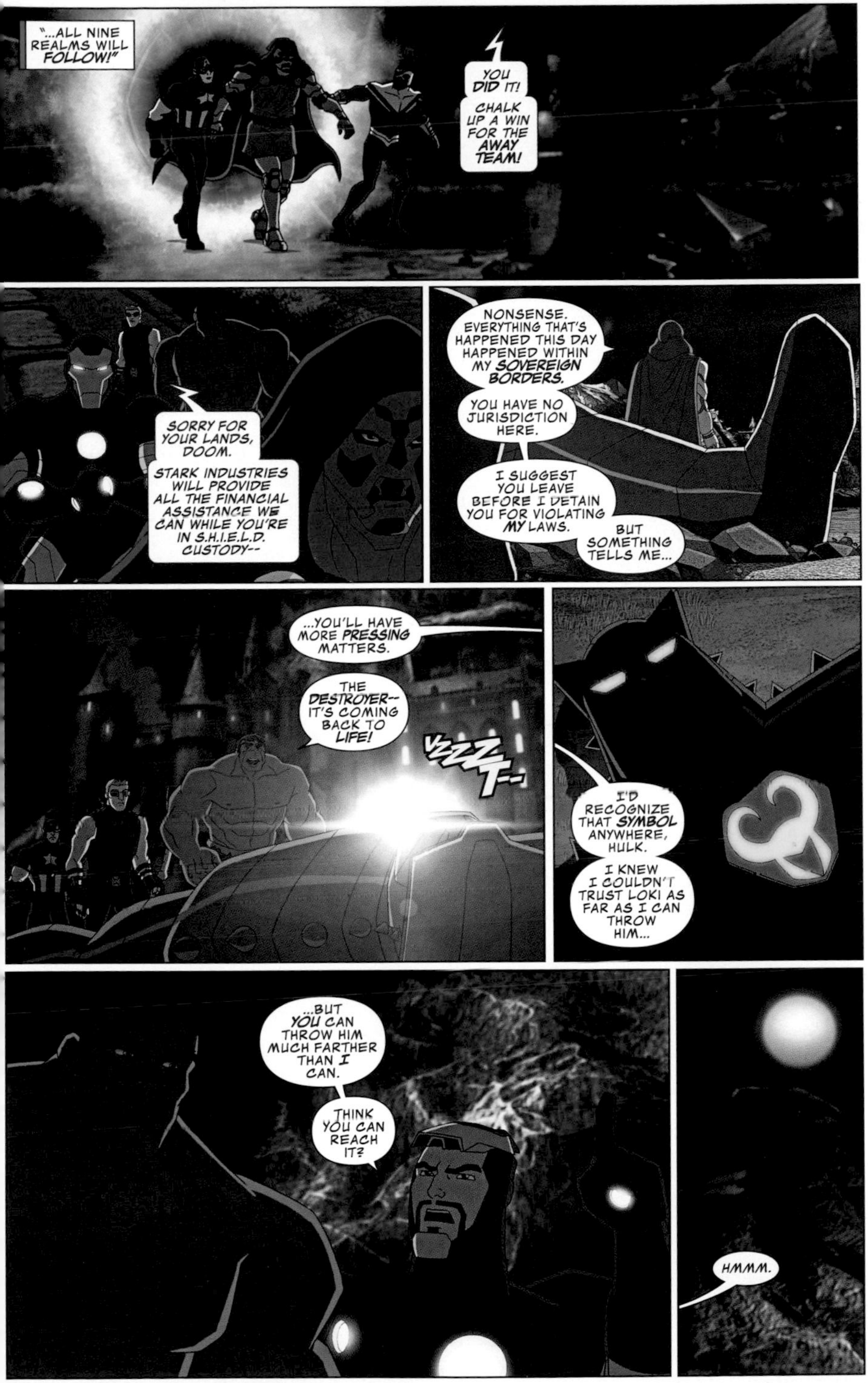
"...ALL NINE REALMS WILL FOLLOW!"
YOU DID IT!
CHALK UP A WIN FOR THE AWAY TEAM!
SORRY FOR YOUR LANDS, DOOM.
STARK INDUSTRIES WILL PROVIDE ALL THE FINANCIAL ASSISTANCE WE CAN WHILE YOU'RE IN S.H.I.E.L.D. CUSTODY--
NONSENSE. EVERYTHING THAT'S HAPPENED THIS DAY HAPPENED WITHIN MY SOVEREIGN BORDERS.
YOU HAVE NO JURISDICTION HERE.
I SUGGEST YOU LEAVE BEFORE I DETAIN YOU FOR VIOLATING MY LAWS.
BUT SOMETHING TELLS ME...
...YOU'LL HAVE MORE PRESSING MATTERS.
THE DESTROYER-- IT'S COMING BACK TO LIFE!
VZZZT--
I'D RECOGNIZE THAT SYMBOL ANYWHERE, HULK.
I KNEW I COULDN'T TRUST LOKI AS FAR AS I CAN THROW HIM...
...BUT YOU CAN THROW HIM MUCH FARTHER THAN I CAN.
THINK YOU CAN REACH IT?
HMMM.

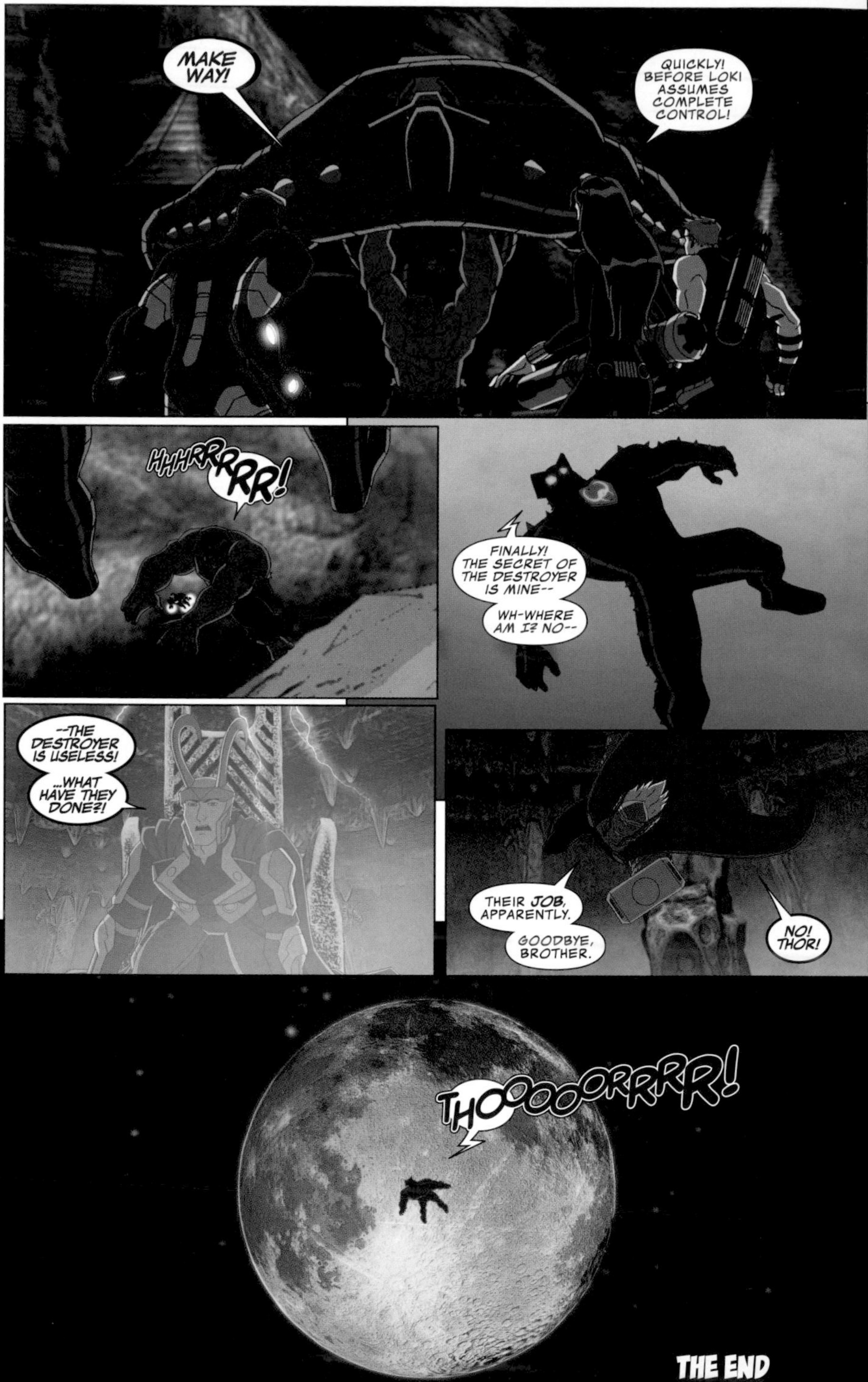
MAKE WAY!
QUICKLY! BEFORE LOKI ASSUMES COMPLETE CONTROL!
HHHRRRRR!
FINALLY! THE SECRET OF THE DESTROYER IS MINE--
WH-WHERE AM I? NO--
--THE DESTROYER IS USELESS!
...WHAT HAVE THEY DONE?!
THEIR JOB, APPARENTLY.
GOODBYE, BROTHER.
NO! THOR!
THOOOOORRRR!
THE END

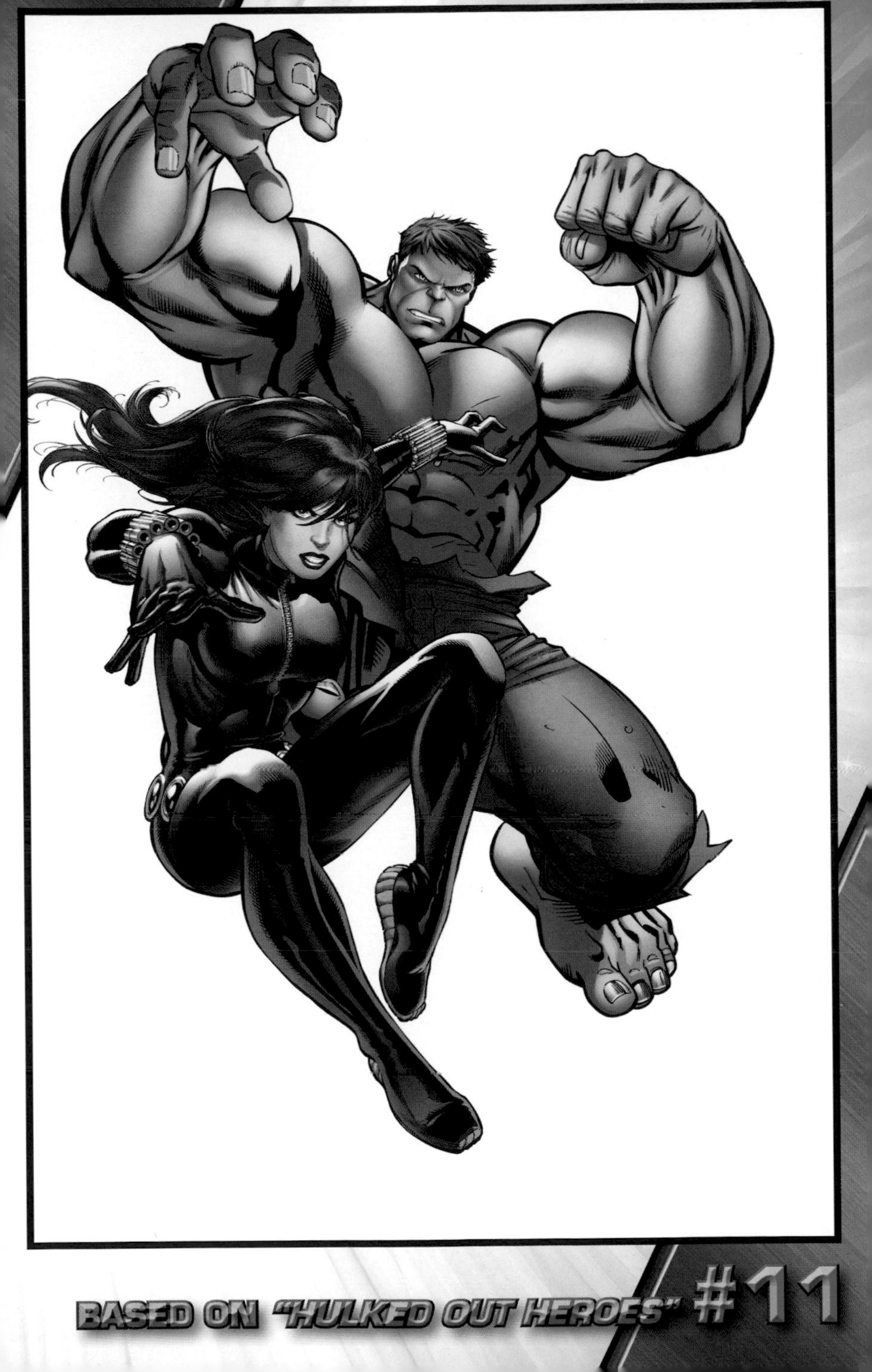

BASED ON "HULKED OUT HEROES" #11

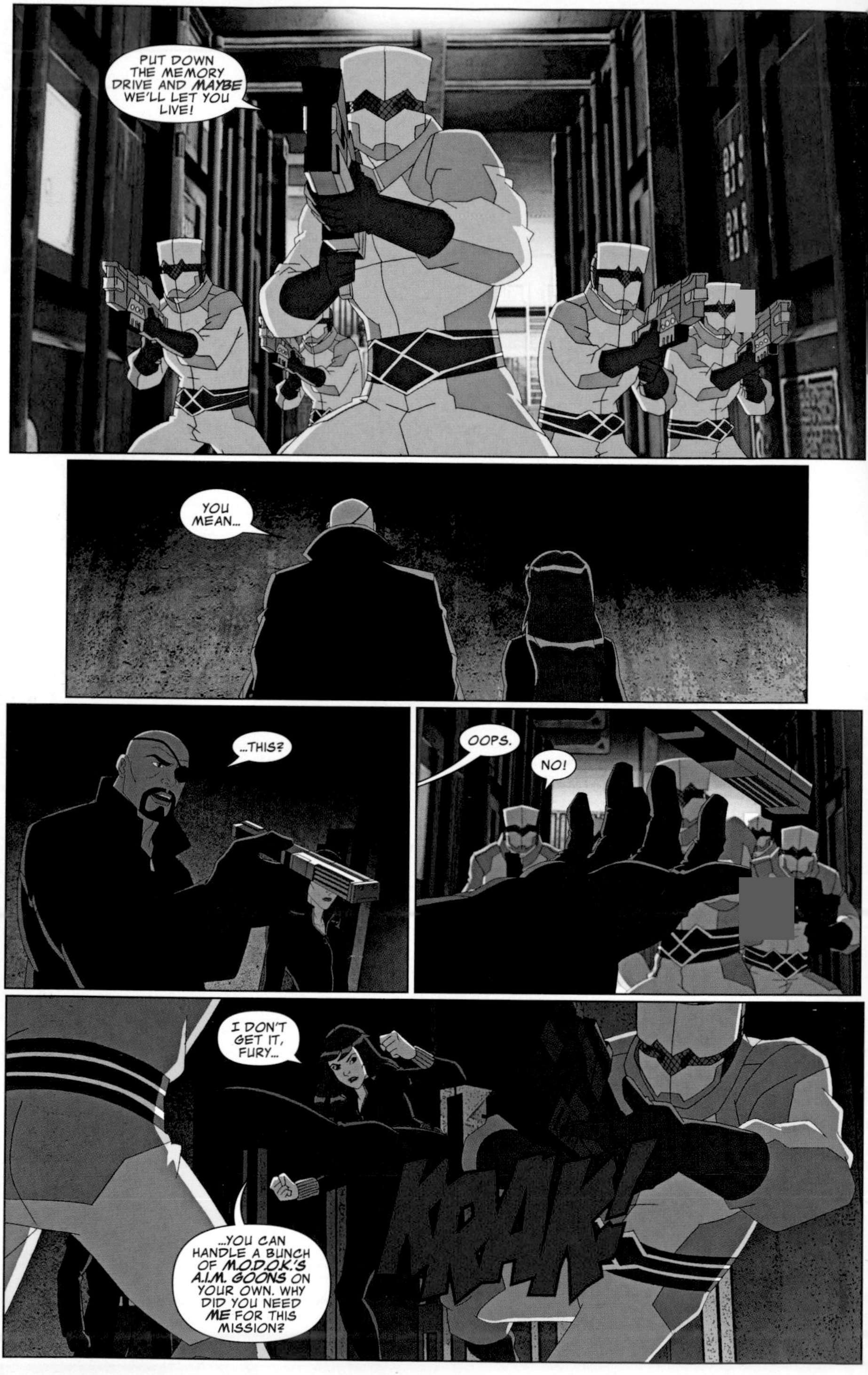

PUT DOWN THE MEMORY DRIVE AND MAYBE WE'LL LET YOU LIVE!
YOU MEAN...
...THIS?
OOPS.
NO!
I DON'T GET IT, FURY...
...YOU CAN HANDLE A BUNCH OF M.O.D.O.K.'S A.I.M. GOONS ON YOUR OWN. WHY DID YOU NEED ME FOR THIS MISSION?

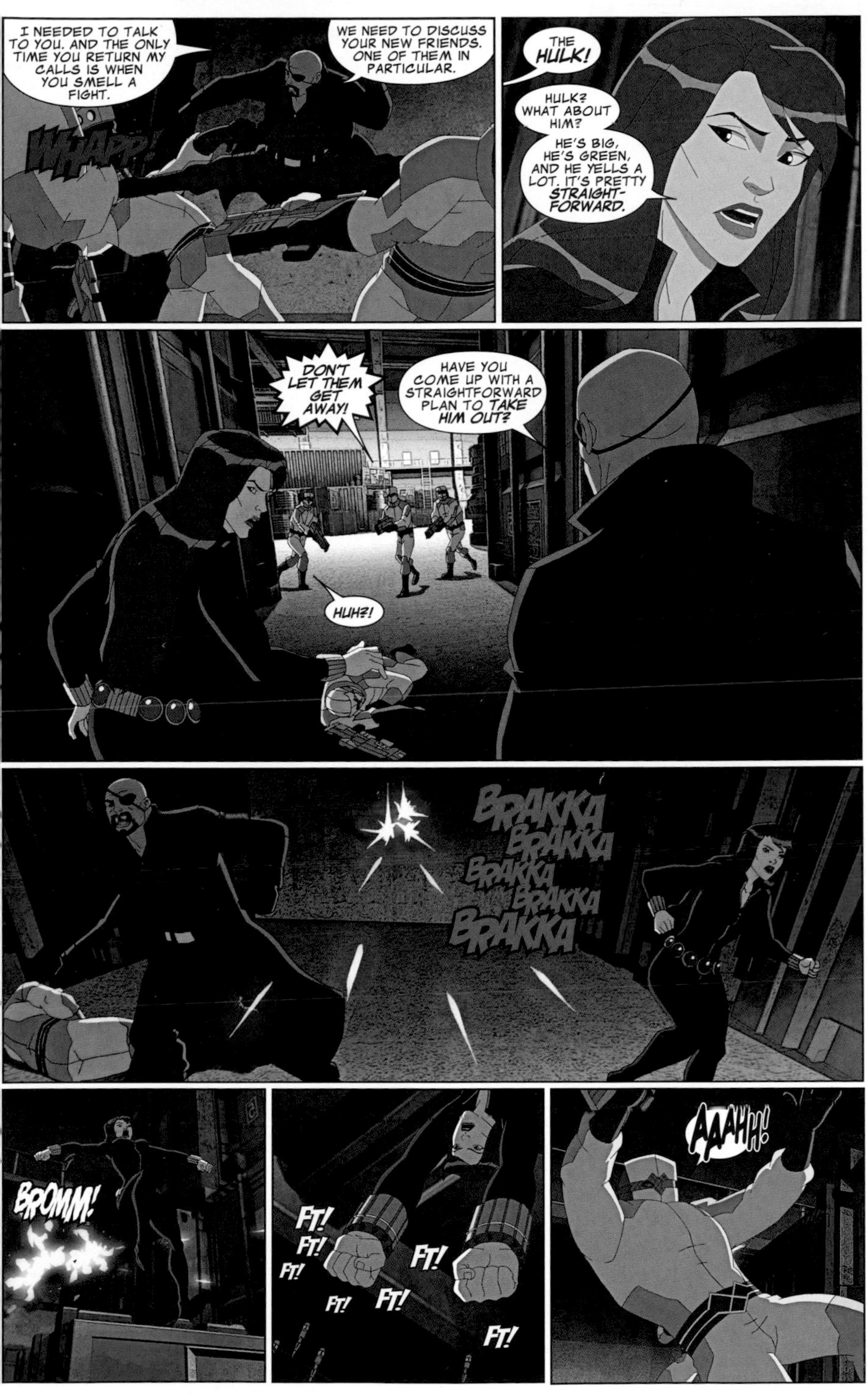
I NEEDED TO TALK TO YOU. AND THE ONLY TIME YOU RETURN MY CALLS IS WHEN YOU SMELL A FIGHT.
WE NEED TO DISCUSS YOUR NEW FRIENDS. ONE OF THEM IN PARTICULAR.
WHAPP!
THE HULK!
HULK? WHAT ABOUT HIM?
HE'S BIG, HE'S GREEN, AND HE YELLS A LOT. IT'S PRETTY STRAIGHTFORWARD.
DON'T LET THEM GET AWAY!
HAVE YOU COME UP WITH A STRAIGHTFORWARD PLAN TO TAKE HIM OUT?
HUH?!
BRAKKA BRAKKA BRAKKA BRAKKA BRAKKA
BROMM!
FT! FT! FT! FT! FT! FT! FT!
AAAHH!

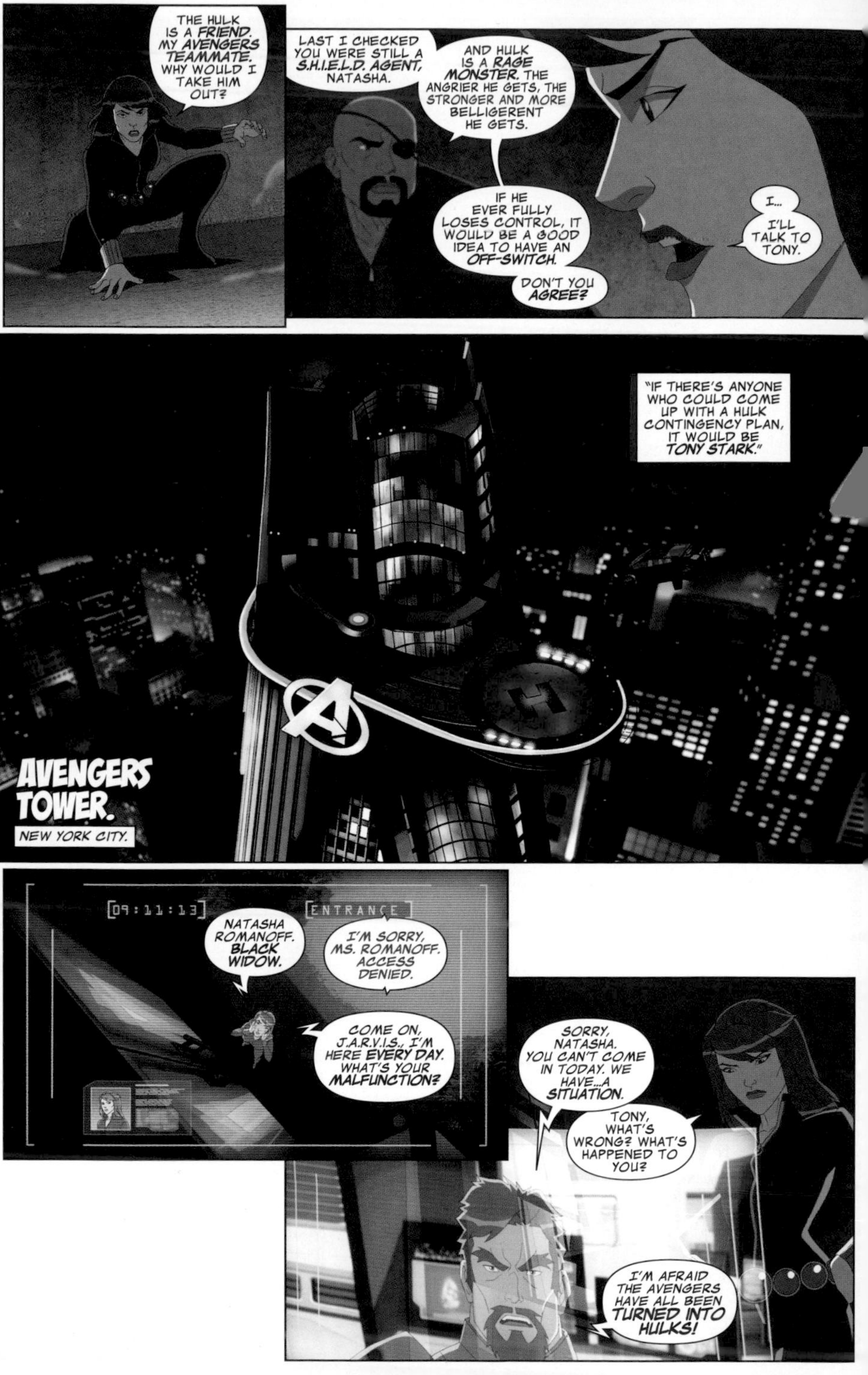
THE HULK IS A FRIEND. MY AVENGERS TEAMMATE. WHY WOULD I TAKE HIM OUT?
LAST I CHECKED YOU WERE STILL A S.H.I.E.L.D. AGENT, NATASHA.
AND HULK IS A RAGE MONSTER. THE ANGRIER HE GETS, THE STRONGER AND MORE BELLIGERENT HE GETS.
IF HE EVER FULLY LOSES CONTROL, IT WOULD BE A GOOD IDEA TO HAVE AN OFF-SWITCH.
DON'T YOU AGREE?
I...
I'LL TALK TO TONY.
"IF THERE'S ANYONE WHO COULD COME UP WITH A HULK CONTINGENCY PLAN, IT WOULD BE TONY STARK."
AVENGERS TOWER.
NEW YORK CITY.
09:11:13
ENTRANCE
NATASHA ROMANOFF. BLACK WIDOW.
I'M SORRY, MS. ROMANOFF. ACCESS DENIED.
COME ON, J.A.R.V.I.S., I'M HERE EVERY DAY. WHAT'S YOUR MALFUNCTION?
SORRY, NATASHA. YOU CAN'T COME IN TODAY. WE HAVE...A SITUATION.
TONY, WHAT'S WRONG? WHAT'S HAPPENED TO YOU?
I'M AFRAID THE AVENGERS HAVE ALL BEEN TURNED INTO HULKS!

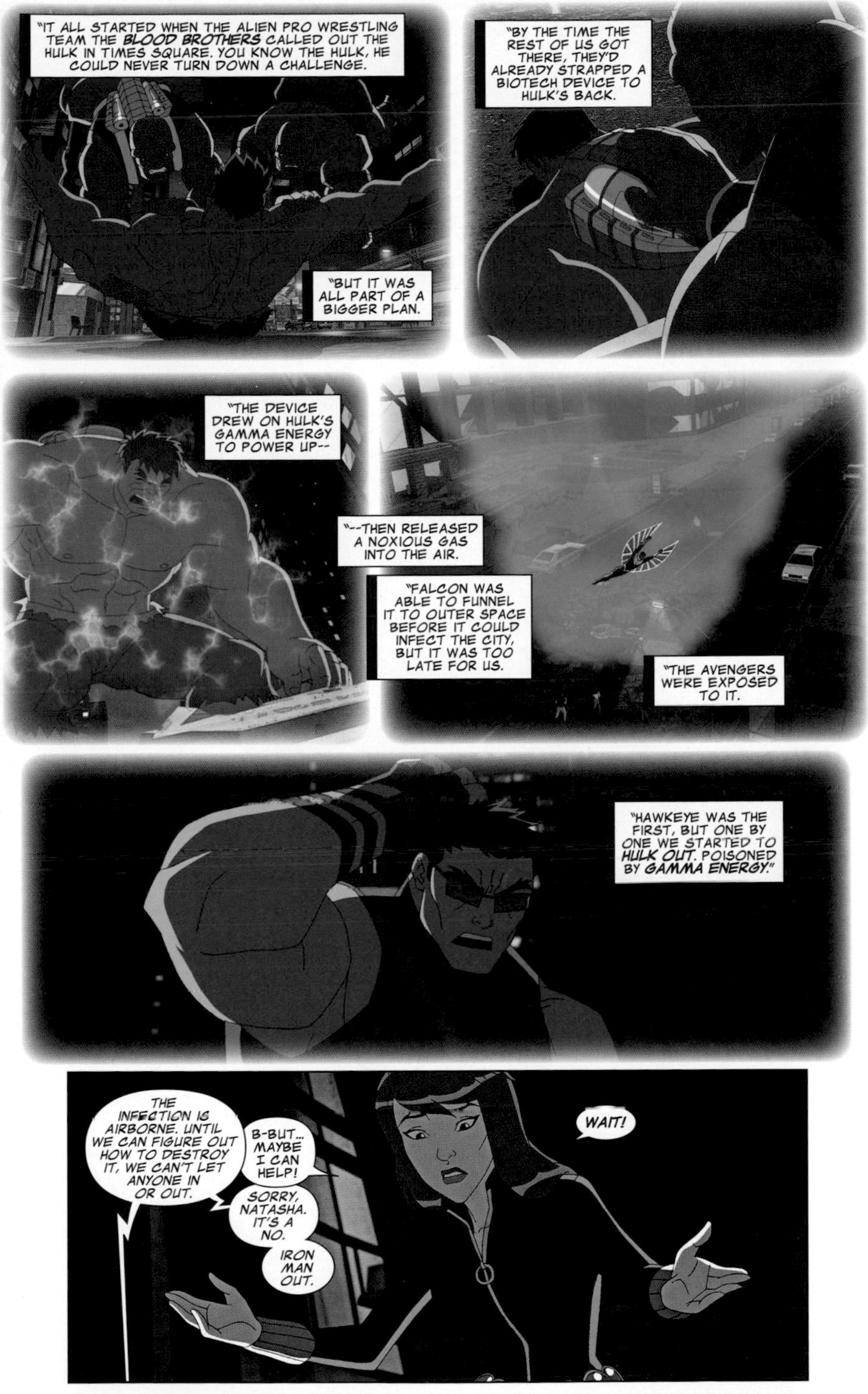
"IT ALL STARTED WHEN THE ALIEN PRO WRESTLING TEAM THE BLOOD BROTHERS CALLED OUT THE HULK IN TIMES SQUARE. YOU KNOW THE HULK, HE COULD NEVER TURN DOWN A CHALLENGE.
"BUT IT WAS ALL PART OF A BIGGER PLAN.
"BY THE TIME THE REST OF US GOT THERE, THEY'D ALREADY STRAPPED A BIOTECH DEVICE TO HULK'S BACK.
"THE DEVICE DREW ON HULK'S GAMMA ENERGY TO POWER UP--
"--THEN RELEASED A NOXIOUS GAS INTO THE AIR.
"FALCON WAS ABLE TO FUNNEL IT TO OUTER SPACE BEFORE IT COULD INFECT THE CITY, BUT IT WAS TOO LATE FOR US.
"THE AVENGERS WERE EXPOSED TO IT.
"HAWKEYE WAS THE FIRST, BUT ONE BY ONE WE STARTED TO HULK OUT. POISONED BY GAMMA ENERGY."
THE INFECTION IS AIRBORNE. UNTIL WE CAN FIGURE OUT HOW TO DESTROY IT, WE CAN'T LET ANYONE IN OR OUT.
B-BUT... MAYBE I CAN HELP!
SORRY, NATASHA. IT'S A NO.
IRON MAN OUT.
WAIT!

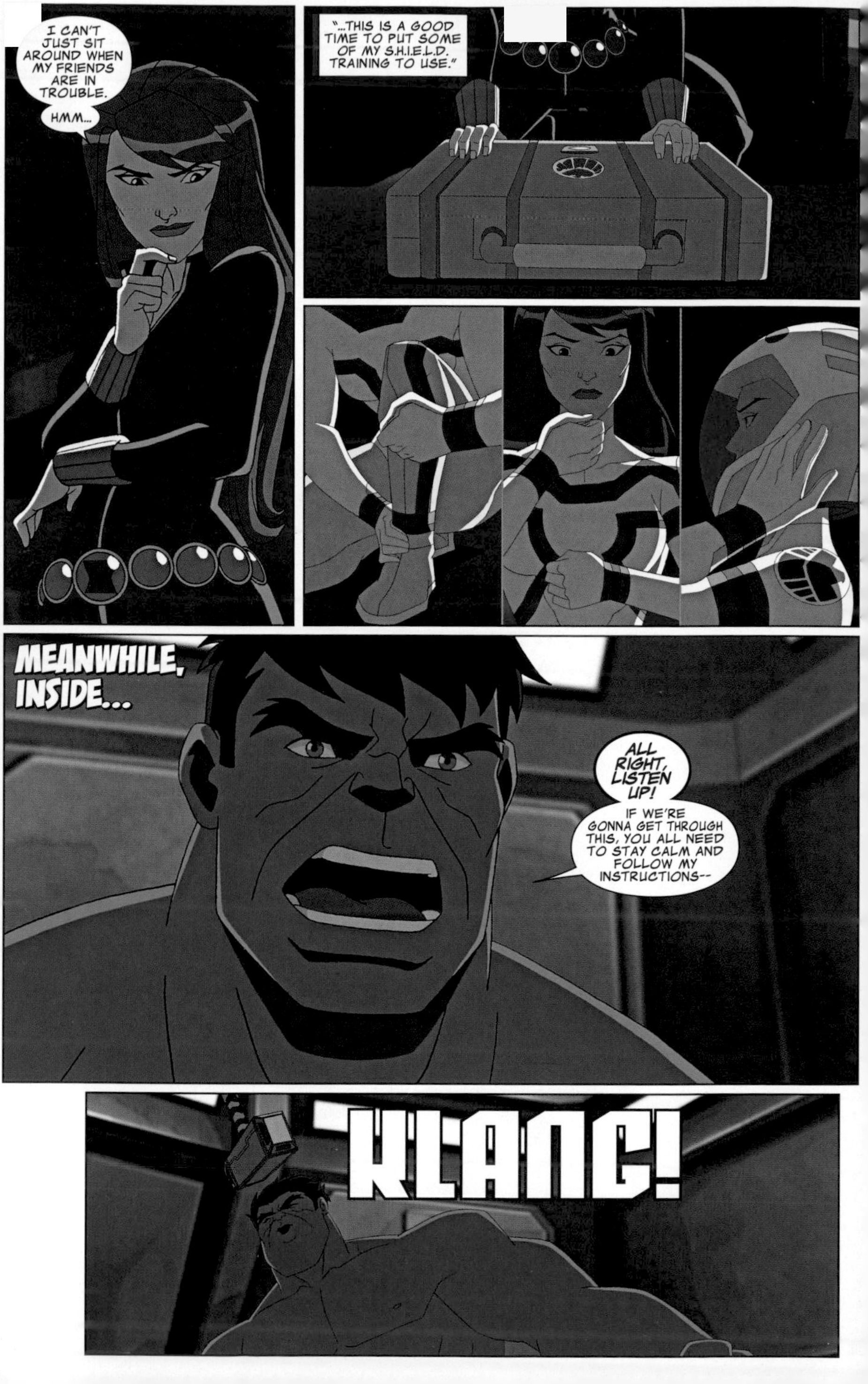
I CAN'T JUST SIT AROUND WHEN MY FRIENDS ARE IN TROUBLE.
HMM...
"...THIS IS A GOOD TIME TO PUT SOME OF MY S.H.I.E.L.D. TRAINING TO USE."
MEANWHILE, INSIDE...
ALL RIGHT, LISTEN UP!
IF WE'RE GONNA GET THROUGH THIS, YOU ALL NEED TO STAY CALM AND FOLLOW MY INSTRUCTIONS--
KLANG!

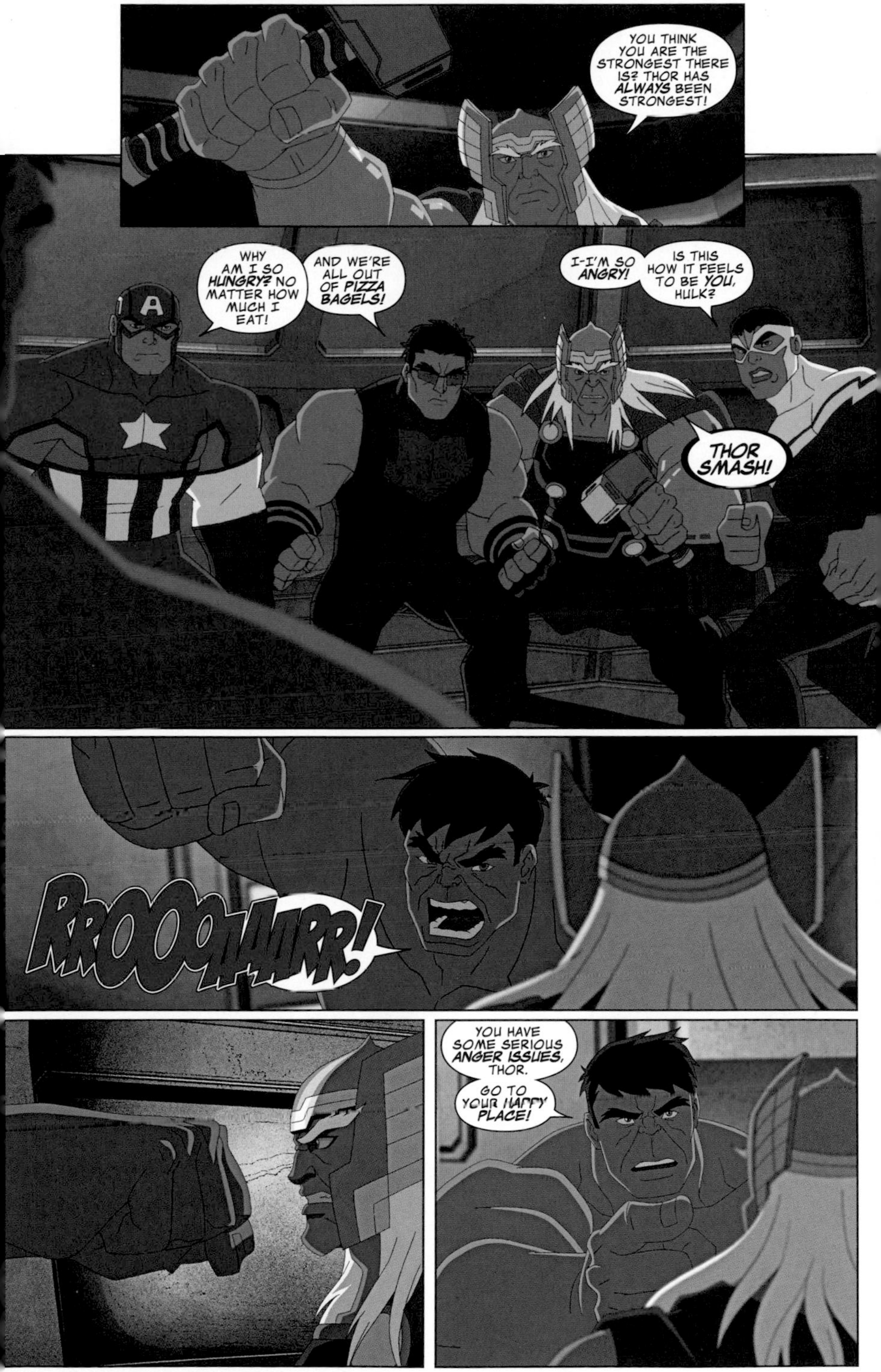
YOU THINK YOU ARE THE STRONGEST THERE IS? THOR HAS ALWAYS BEEN STRONGEST!
WHY AM I SO HUNGRY? NO MATTER HOW MUCH I EAT!
AND WE'RE ALL OUT OF PIZZA BAGELS!
I-I'M SO ANGRY!
IS THIS HOW IT FEELS TO BE YOU, HULK?
THOR SMASH!
RROOOWARR!
YOU HAVE SOME SERIOUS ANGER ISSUES, THOR.
GO TO YOUR HAPPY PLACE!

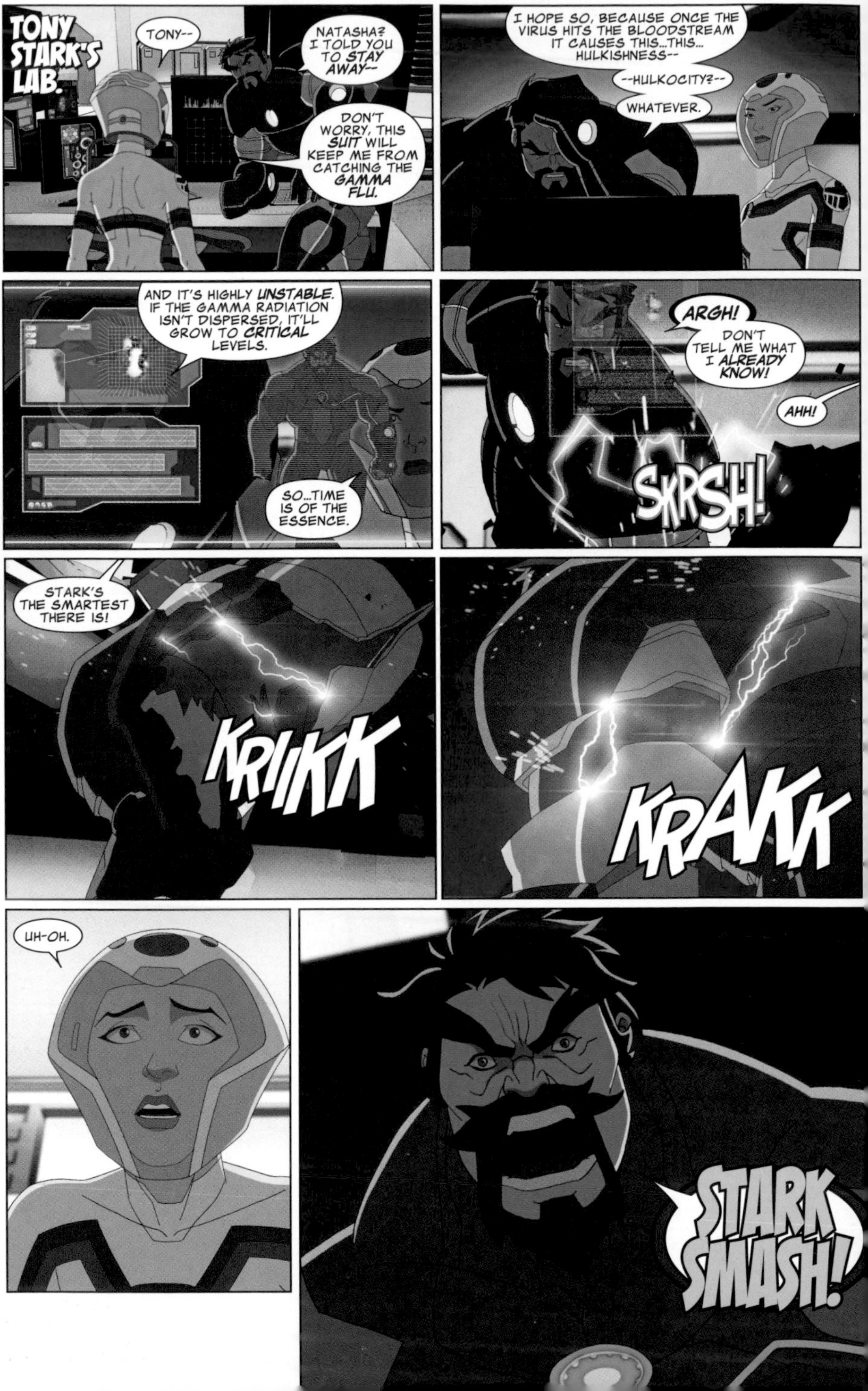
TONY STARK'S LAB.
TONY--
NATASHA? I TOLD YOU TO STAY AWAY--
DON'T WORRY, THIS SUIT WILL KEEP ME FROM CATCHING THE GAMMA FLU.
I HOPE SO, BECAUSE ONCE THE VIRUS HITS THE BLOODSTREAM IT CAUSES THIS...THIS... HULKISHNESS--
--HULKOCITY?--
WHATEVER.
AND IT'S HIGHLY UNSTABLE. IF THE GAMMA RADIATION ISN'T DISPERSED, IT'LL GROW TO CRITICAL LEVELS.
SO...TIME IS OF THE ESSENCE.
ARGH!
DON'T TELL ME WHAT I ALREADY KNOW!
AHH!
SKRSH!
STARK'S THE SMARTEST THERE IS!
KRIIKK
KRAKK
UH-OH.
STARK SMASH!

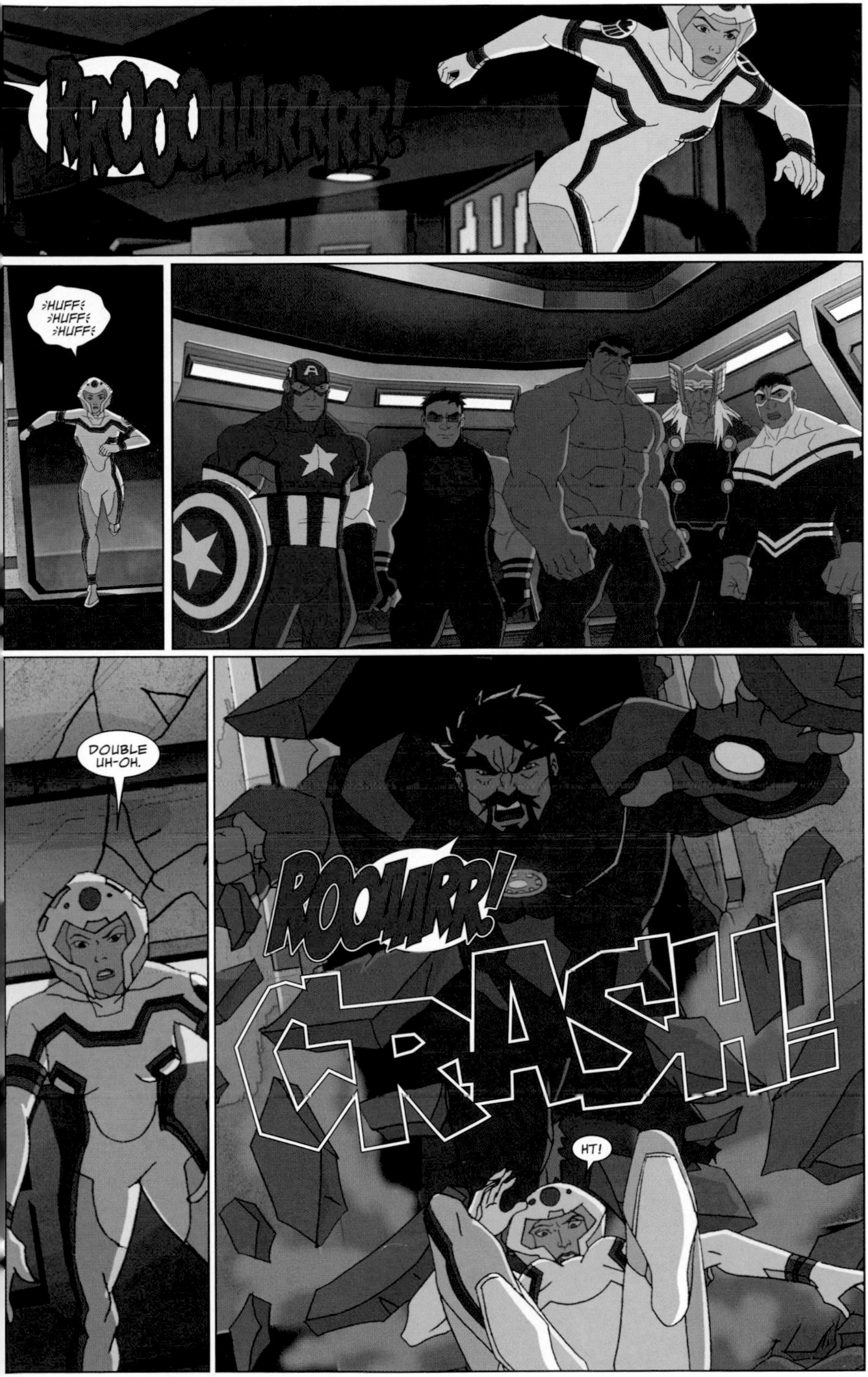
RROOOOWRRRRR!
HUFF
HUFF
HUFF
DOUBLE UH-OH.
ROOWRR!
CRASH!
HT!

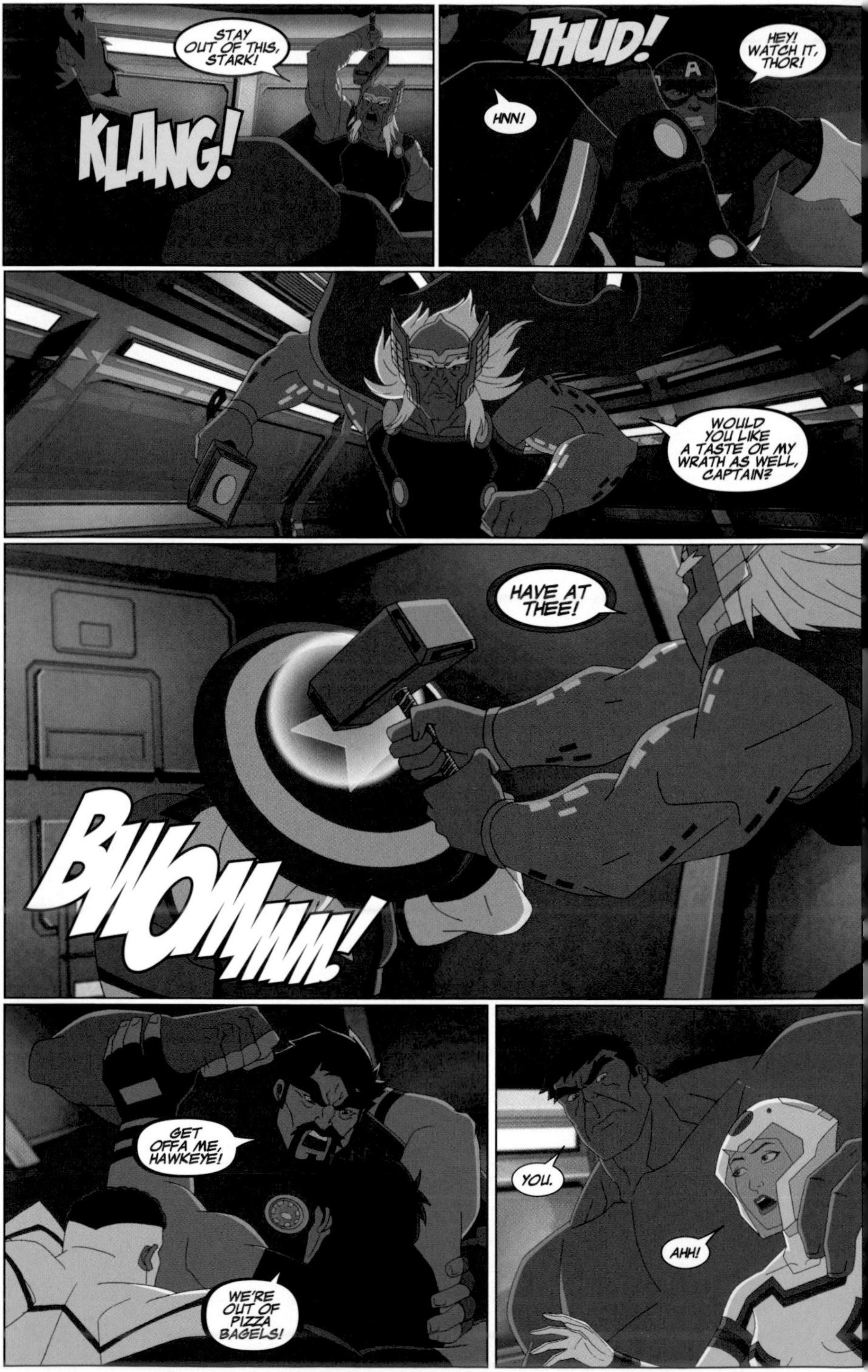
STAY OUT OF THIS, STARK!
KLANG!
THUD!
HEY! WATCH IT, THOR!
HNN!
WOULD YOU LIKE A TASTE OF MY WRATH AS WELL, CAPTAIN?
HAVE AT THEE!
BWOMMM!
GET OFFA ME, HAWKEYE!
WE'RE OUT OF PIZZA BAGELS!
YOU.
AHH!

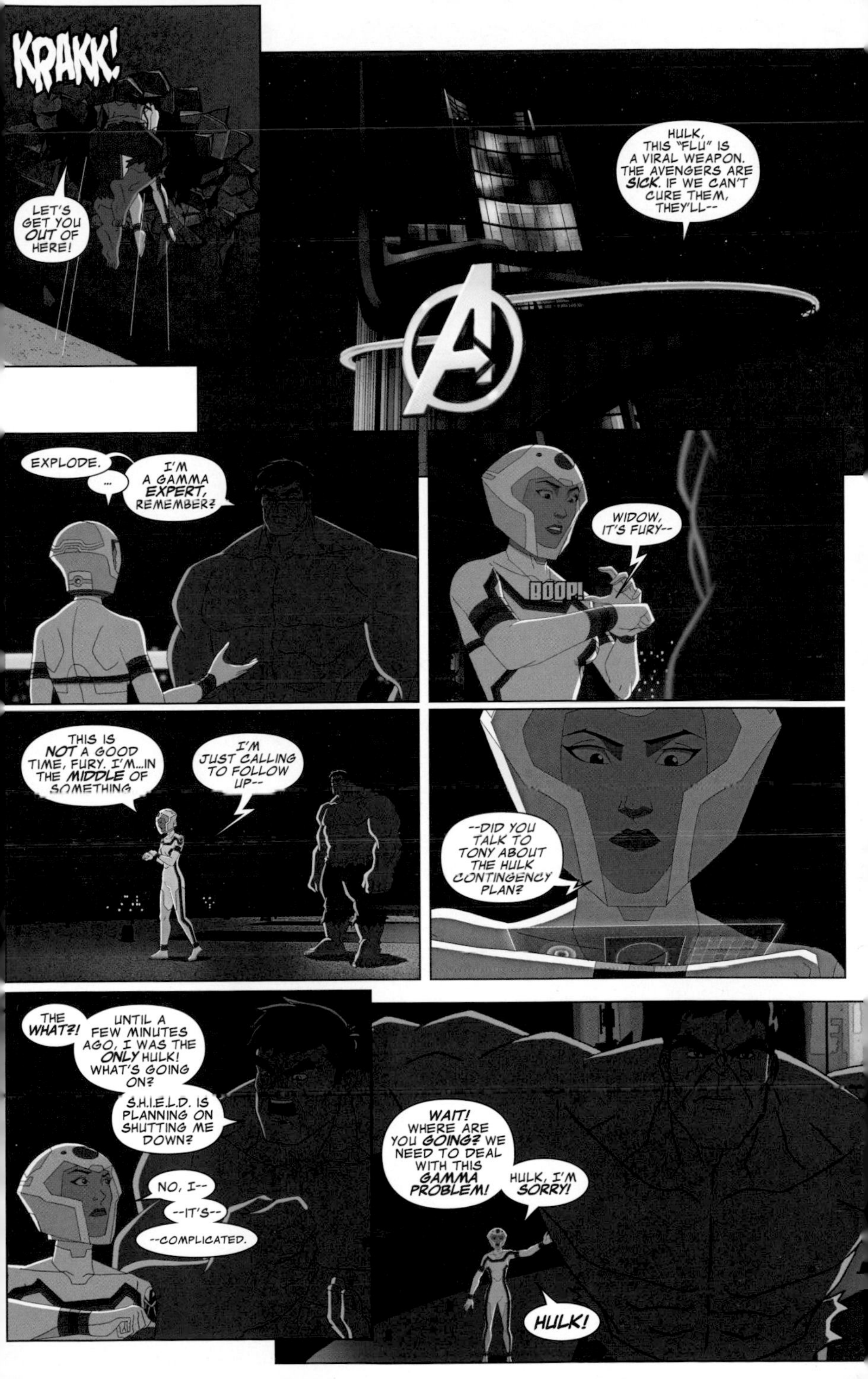
KRAKK!
LET'S GET YOU OUT OF HERE!
HULK, THIS "FLU" IS A VIRAL WEAPON. THE AVENGERS ARE SICK. IF WE CAN'T CURE THEM, THEY'LL--
EXPLODE.
...
I'M A GAMMA EXPERT, REMEMBER?
WIDOW, IT'S FURY--
BOOP!
THIS IS NOT A GOOD TIME, FURY. I'M...IN THE MIDDLE OF SOMETHING
I'M JUST CALLING TO FOLLOW UP--
--DID YOU TALK TO TONY ABOUT THE HULK CONTINGENCY PLAN?
THE WHAT?!
UNTIL A FEW MINUTES AGO, I WAS THE ONLY HULK! WHAT'S GOING ON?
S.H.I.E.L.D. IS PLANNING ON SHUTTING ME DOWN?
NO, I--
--IT'S--
--COMPLICATED.
WAIT! WHERE ARE YOU GOING? WE NEED TO DEAL WITH THIS GAMMA PROBLEM!
HULK, I'M SORRY!
HULK!

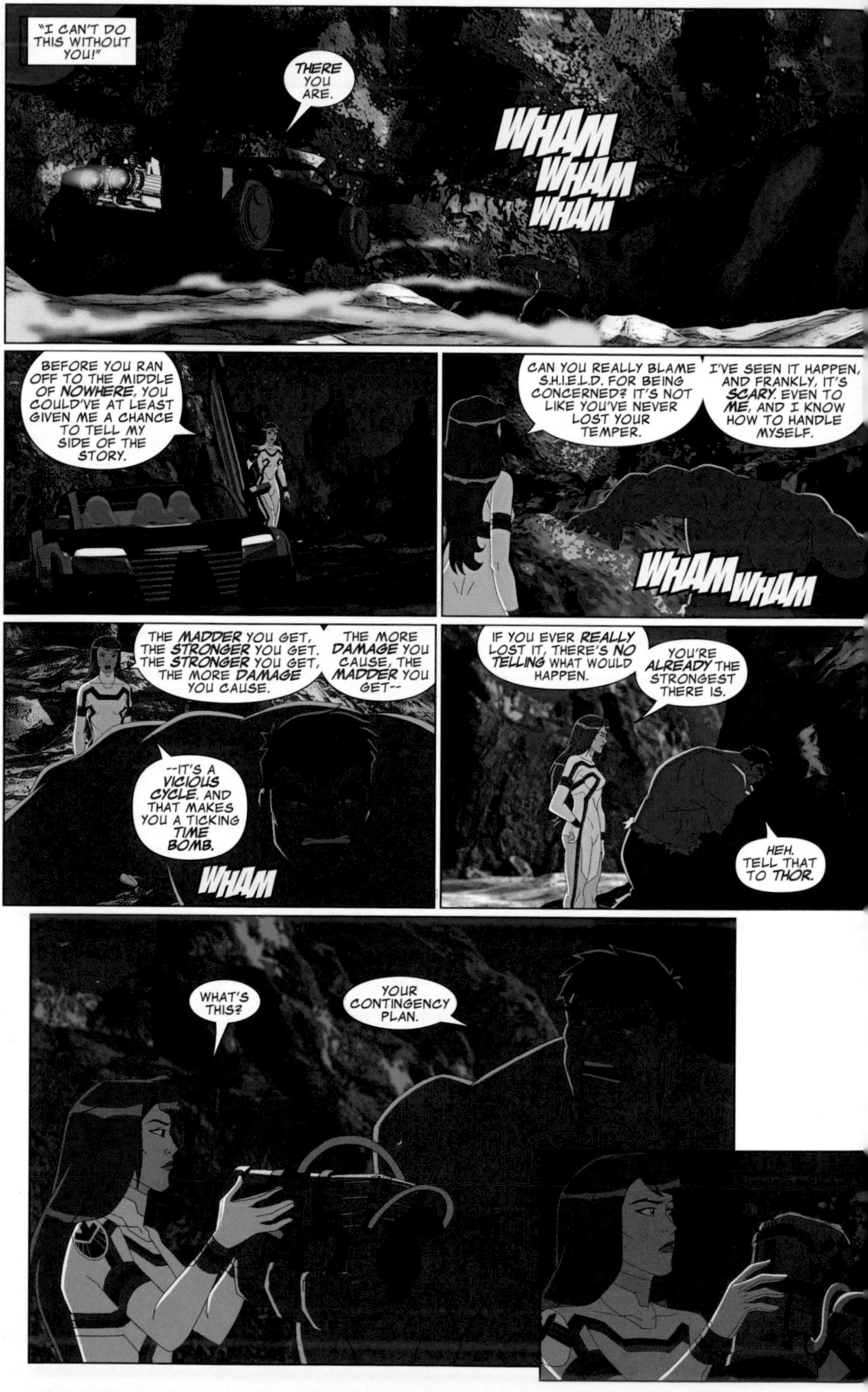
"I CAN'T DO THIS WITHOUT YOU!"
THERE YOU ARE.
WHAM WHAM WHAM
BEFORE YOU RAN OFF TO THE MIDDLE OF NOWHERE, YOU COULD'VE AT LEAST GIVEN ME A CHANCE TO TELL MY SIDE OF THE STORY.
CAN YOU REALLY BLAME S.H.I.E.L.D. FOR BEING CONCERNED? IT'S NOT LIKE YOU'VE NEVER LOST YOUR TEMPER.
I'VE SEEN IT HAPPEN, AND FRANKLY, IT'S SCARY. EVEN TO ME, AND I KNOW HOW TO HANDLE MYSELF.
WHAM WHAM
THE MADDER YOU GET, THE STRONGER YOU GET. THE STRONGER YOU GET, THE MORE DAMAGE YOU CAUSE.
THE MORE DAMAGE YOU CAUSE, THE MADDER YOU GET--
--IT'S A VICIOUS CYCLE. AND THAT MAKES YOU A TICKING TIME BOMB.
WHAM
IF YOU EVER REALLY LOST IT, THERE'S NO TELLING WHAT WOULD HAPPEN.
YOU'RE ALREADY THE STRONGEST THERE IS.
HEH. TELL THAT TO THOR.
WHAT'S THIS?
YOUR CONTINGENCY PLAN.

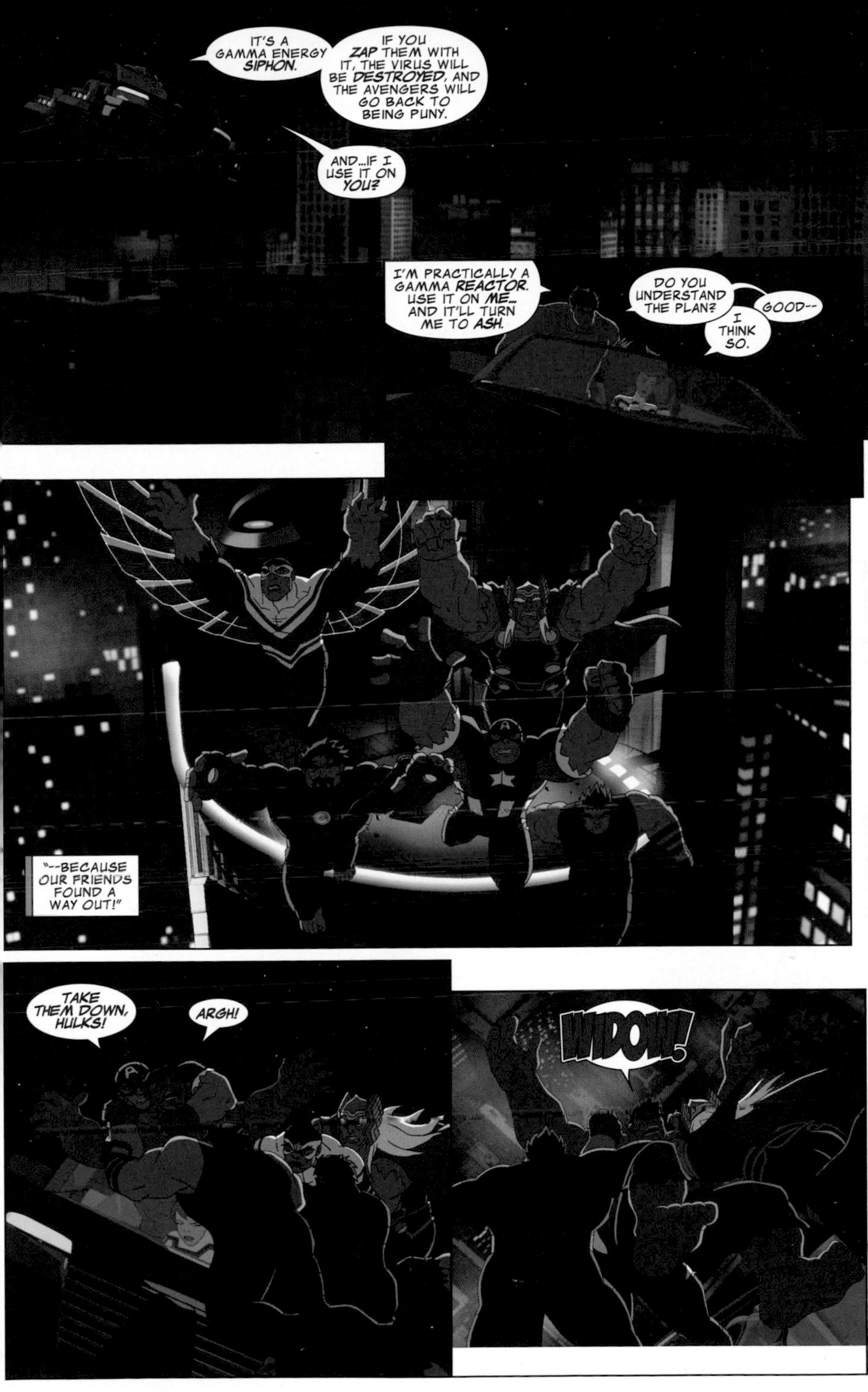
IT'S A GAMMA ENERGY SIPHON.
IF YOU ZAP THEM WITH IT, THE VIRUS WILL BE DESTROYED, AND THE AVENGERS WILL GO BACK TO BEING PUNY.
AND...IF I USE IT ON YOU?
I'M PRACTICALLY A GAMMA REACTOR. USE IT ON ME... AND IT'LL TURN ME TO ASH.
DO YOU UNDERSTAND THE PLAN?
I THINK SO.
GOOD--
"--BECAUSE OUR FRIENDS FOUND A WAY OUT!"
TAKE THEM DOWN, HULKS!
ARGH!
WIDOW!

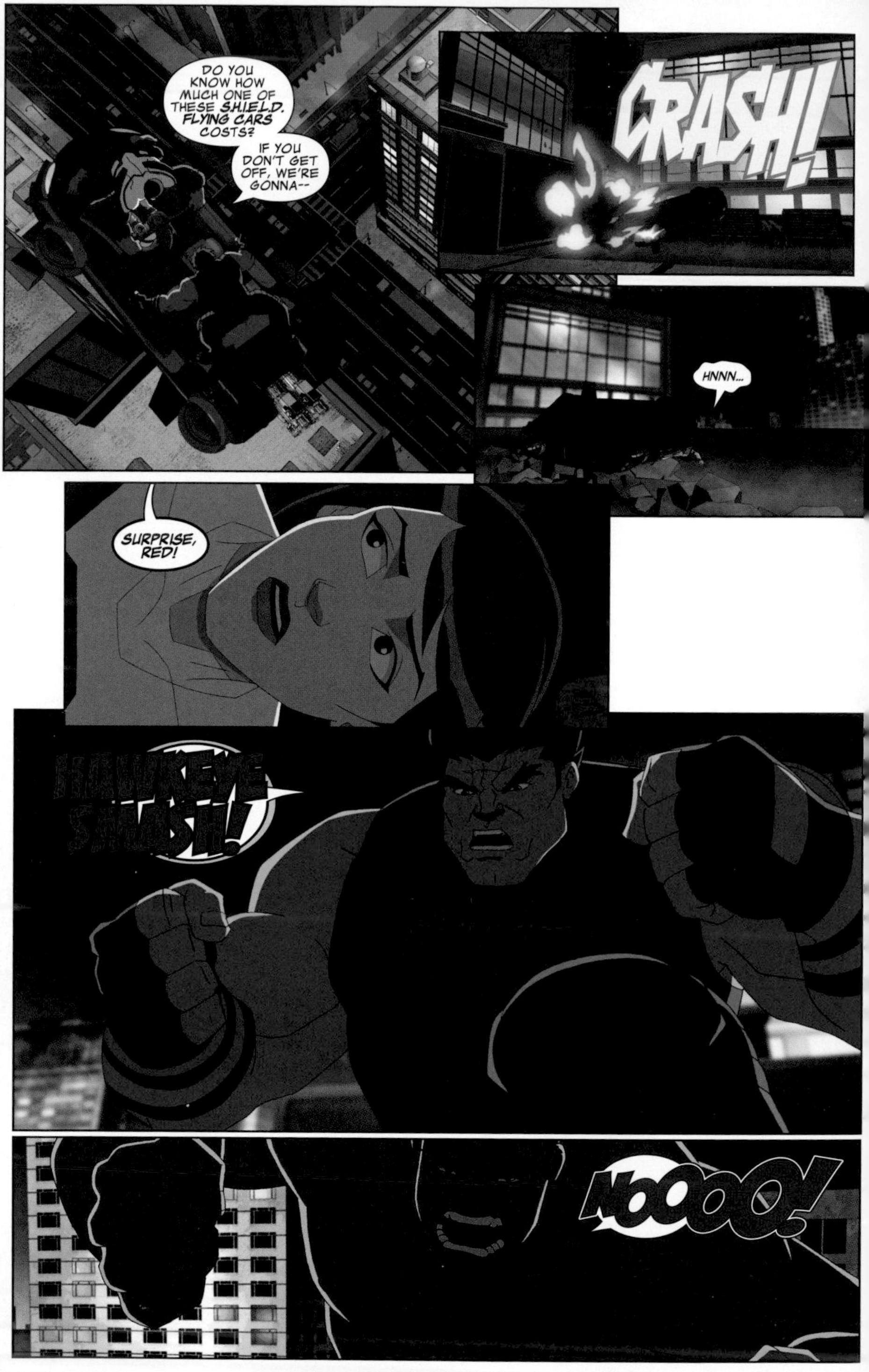
DO YOU KNOW HOW MUCH ONE OF THESE S.H.I.E.L.D. FLYING CARS COSTS?
IF YOU DON'T GET OFF, WE'RE GONNA--
CRASH!
HNNN...
SURPRISE, RED!
HAWKEYE SMASH!
NOOOO!

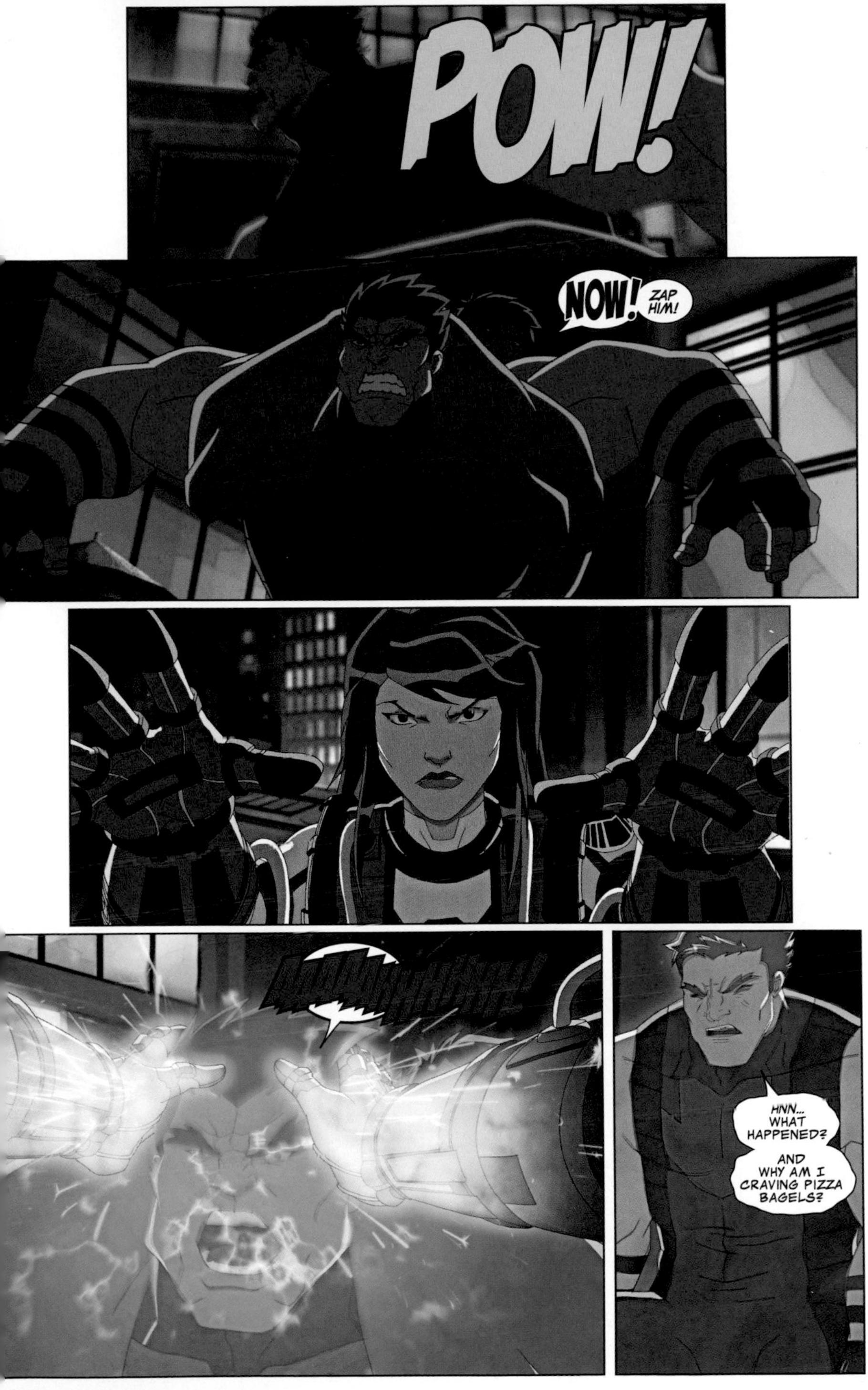
POW!
NOW!
ZAP HIM!
HNN... WHAT HAPPENED?
AND WHY AM I CRAVING PIZZA BAGELS?

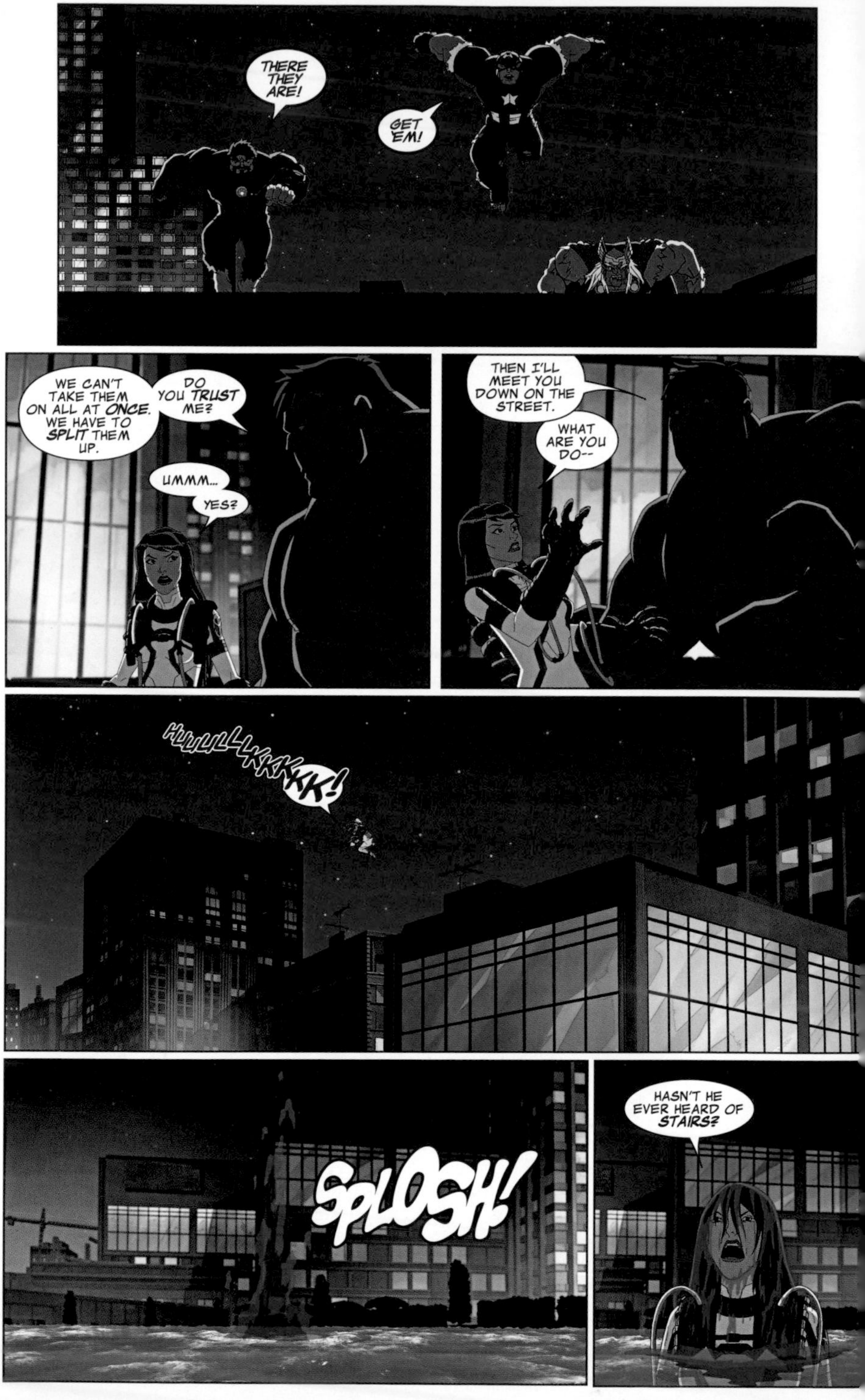
THERE THEY ARE!
GET 'EM!
WE CAN'T TAKE THEM ON ALL AT ONCE. WE HAVE TO SPLIT THEM UP.
DO YOU TRUST ME?
UMMM... YES?
THEN I'LL MEET YOU DOWN ON THE STREET.
WHAT ARE YOU DO--
HUULLLLKKKKKK!
SPLOSH!
HASN'T HE EVER HEARD OF STAIRS?

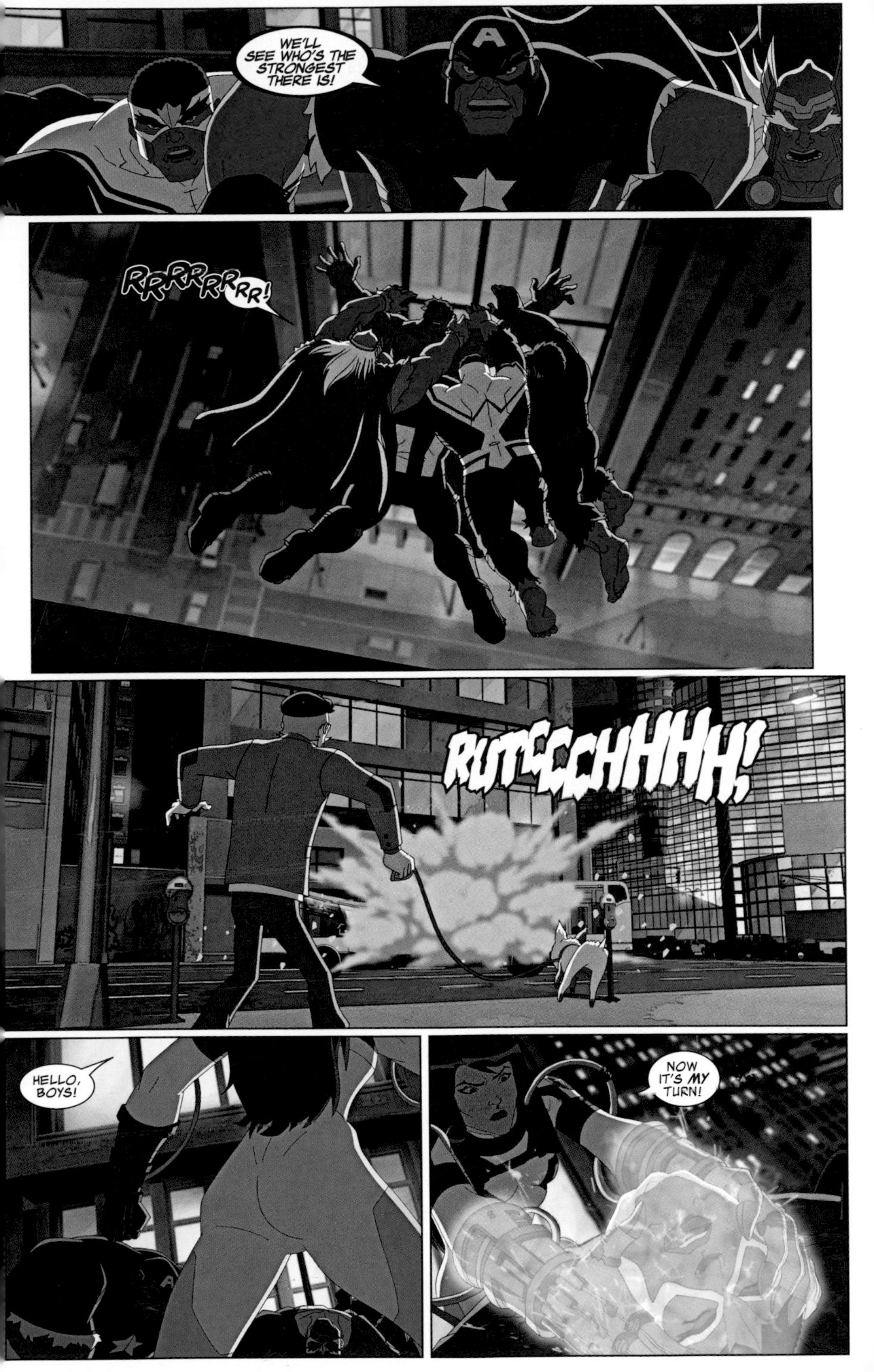
WE'LL SEE WHO'S THE STRONGEST THERE IS!
RRRRRRRRR!
RUTSCCHHHH!
HELLO, BOYS!
NOW IT'S MY TURN!

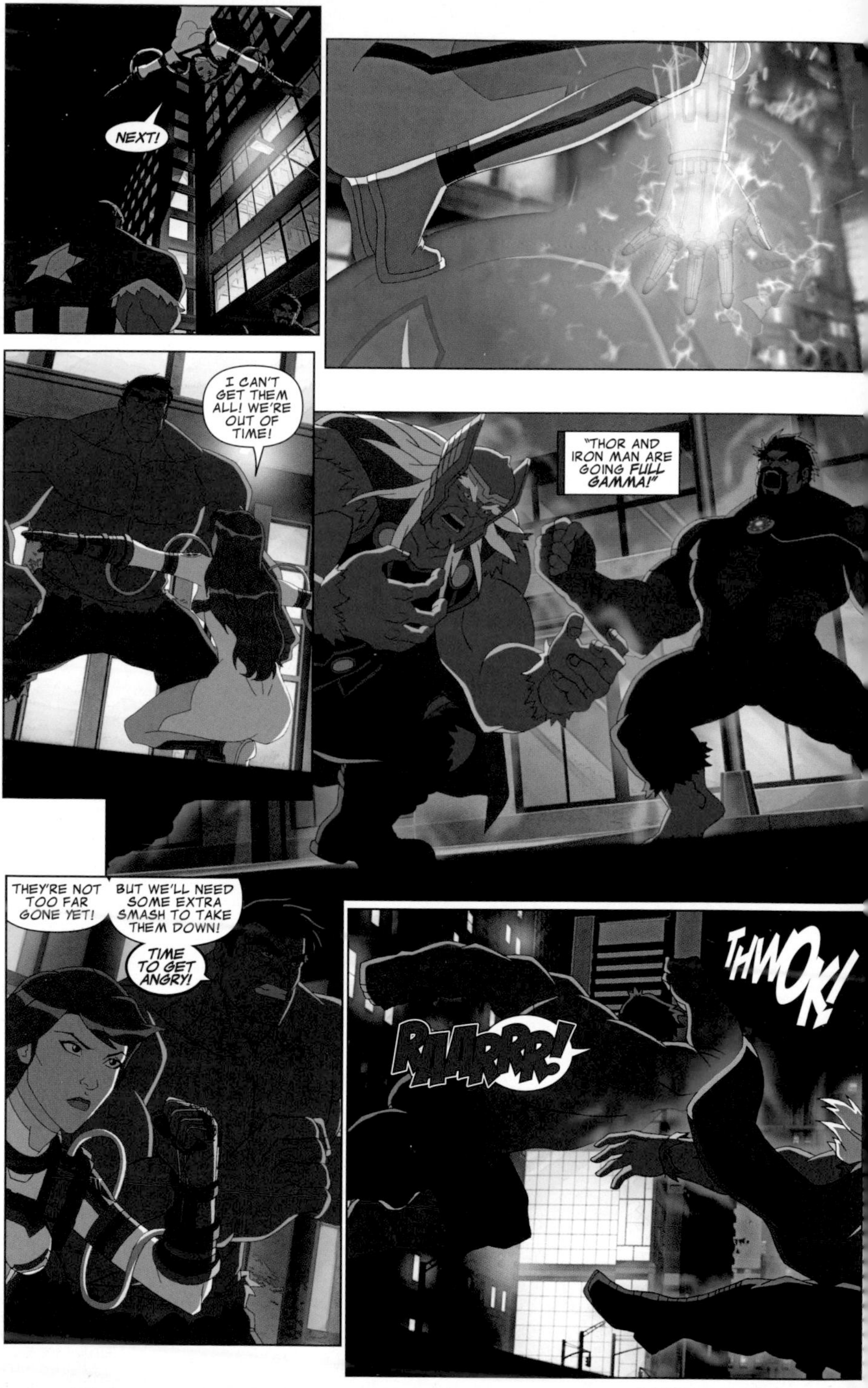
NEXT!
I CAN'T GET THEM ALL! WE'RE OUT OF TIME!
"THOR AND IRON MAN ARE GOING FULL GAMMA!"
THEY'RE NOT TOO FAR GONE YET!
BUT WE'LL NEED SOME EXTRA SMASH TO TAKE THEM DOWN!
TIME TO GET ANGRY!
THWOK!
RWARRR!

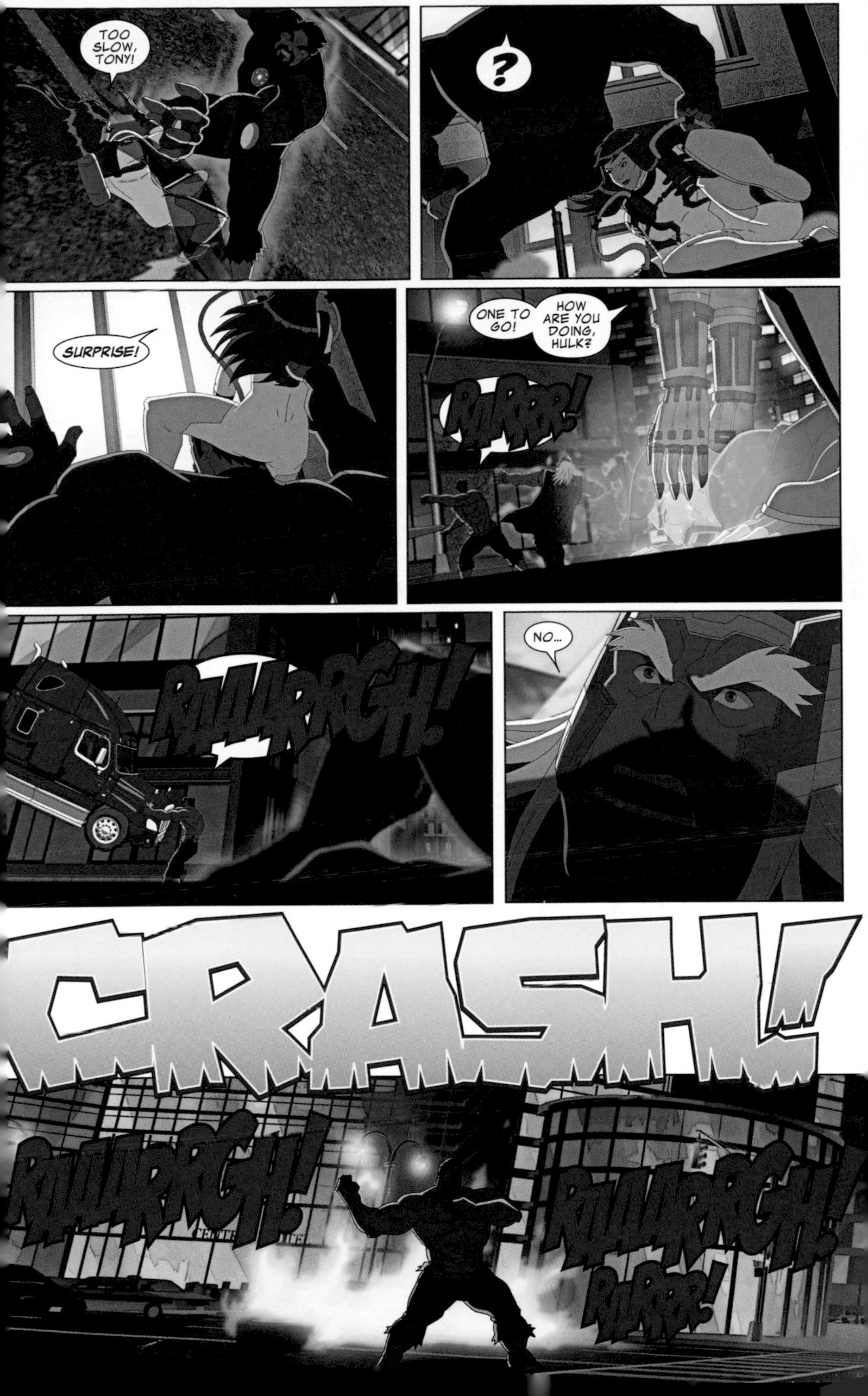
TOO SLOW, TONY!
?
SURPRISE!
ONE TO GO!
HOW ARE YOU DOING, HULK?
RURRR!
RUUURRGH!
NO...
CRASH!
RUUURRGH!
RUUURRGH!
RURRR!

HULK! AM STRONGGGESSST!

DO YOUR THING, WIDOW.

YOU SAW!

YOU'RE MY WITNESS!

I TOTALLY BEAT UP THOR!

I AM THE STRONGEST THERE IS!

HE OWES ME FIVE DOLLARS!

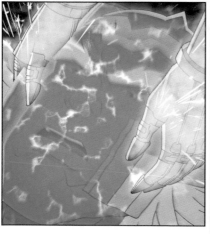

THAT WAS EASY. THANKS TO YOU.

I'M SURE GLAD YOU'RE ON OUR SIDE, HULK.

YOU'RE NOT SO BAD YOURSELF.

"WALK ME THROUGH THIS AGAIN. ONE MORE TIME..."

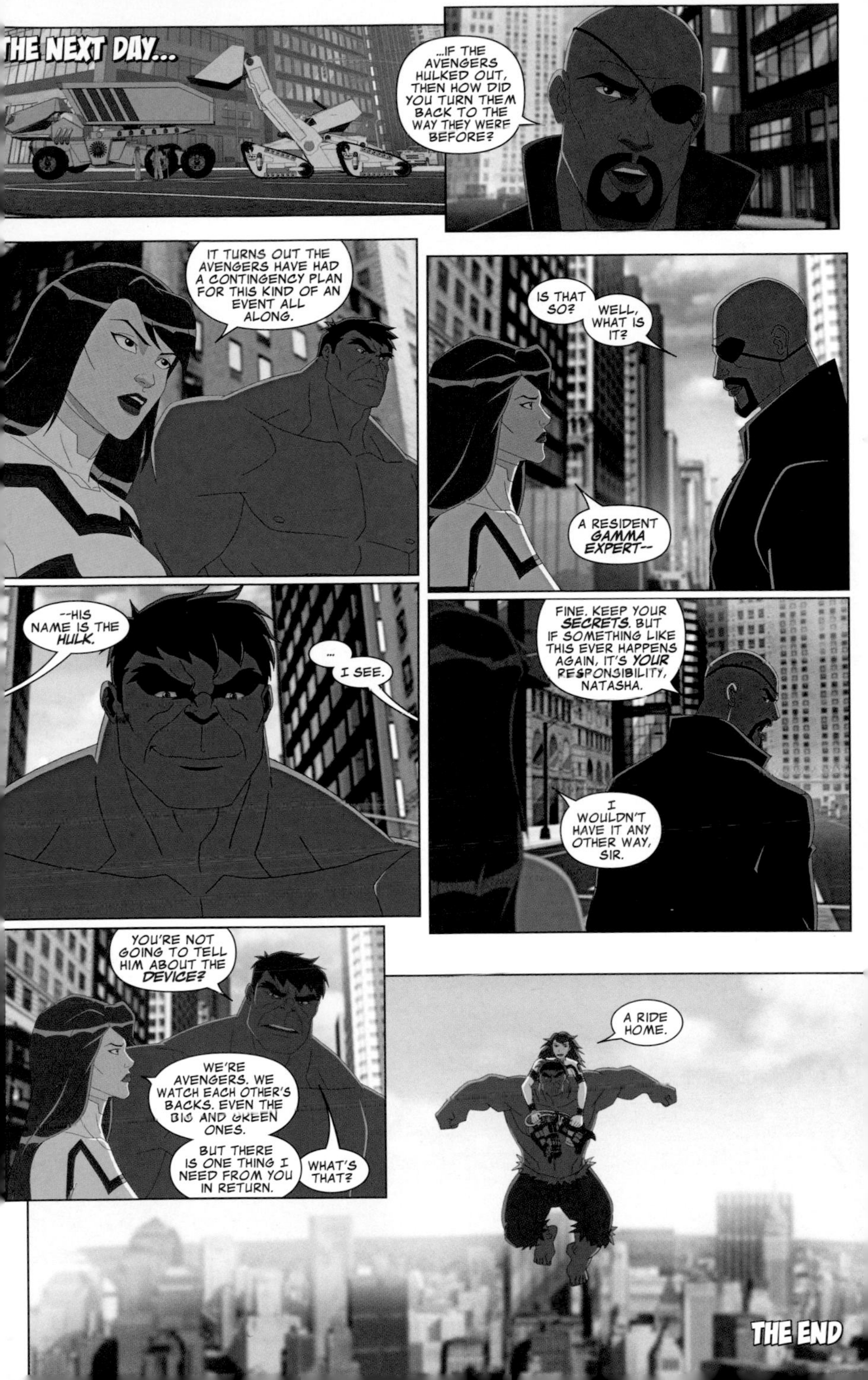
THE NEXT DAY...
...IF THE AVENGERS HULKED OUT, THEN HOW DID YOU TURN THEM BACK TO THE WAY THEY WERE BEFORE?
IT TURNS OUT THE AVENGERS HAVE HAD A CONTINGENCY PLAN FOR THIS KIND OF AN EVENT ALL ALONG.
IS THAT SO?
WELL, WHAT IS IT?
A RESIDENT GAMMA EXPERT--
--HIS NAME IS THE HULK.
... I SEE.
FINE. KEEP YOUR SECRETS. BUT IF SOMETHING LIKE THIS EVER HAPPENS AGAIN, IT'S YOUR RESPONSIBILITY, NATASHA.
I WOULDN'T HAVE IT ANY OTHER WAY, SIR.
YOU'RE NOT GOING TO TELL HIM ABOUT THE DEVICE?
WE'RE AVENGERS. WE WATCH EACH OTHER'S BACKS. EVEN THE BIG AND GREEN ONES.
BUT THERE IS ONE THING I NEED FROM YOU IN RETURN.
WHAT'S THAT?
A RIDE HOME.
THE END

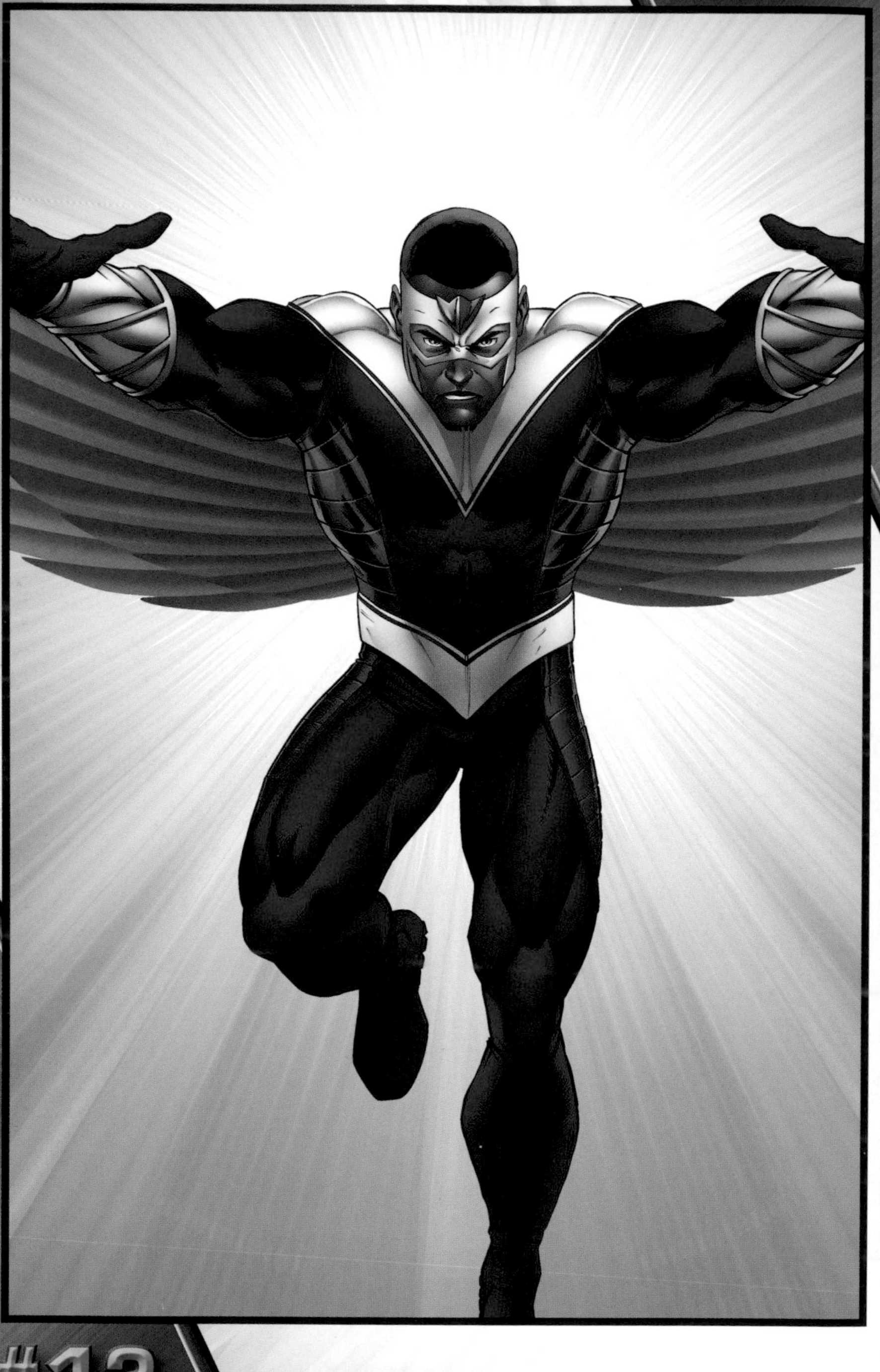

#12 BASED ON "AVENGERS IMPOSSIBLE"

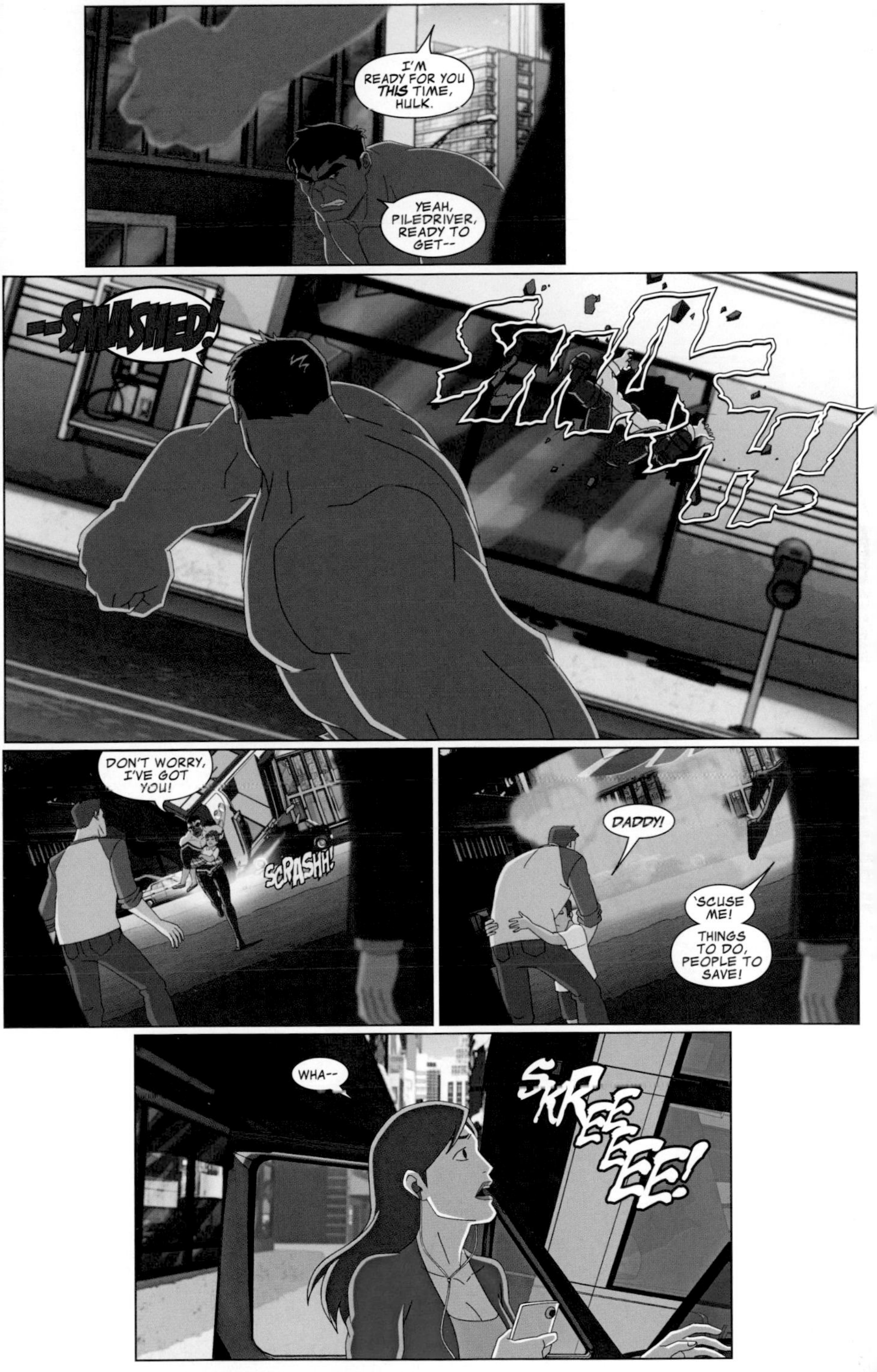
I'M READY FOR YOU THIS TIME, HULK.
YEAH, PILEDRIVER, READY TO GET--
--SMASHED!
DON'T WORRY, I'VE GOT YOU!
SCRASHH!
DADDY!
'SCUSE ME!
THINGS TO DO, PEOPLE TO SAVE!
WHA--
SKREEEEEE!

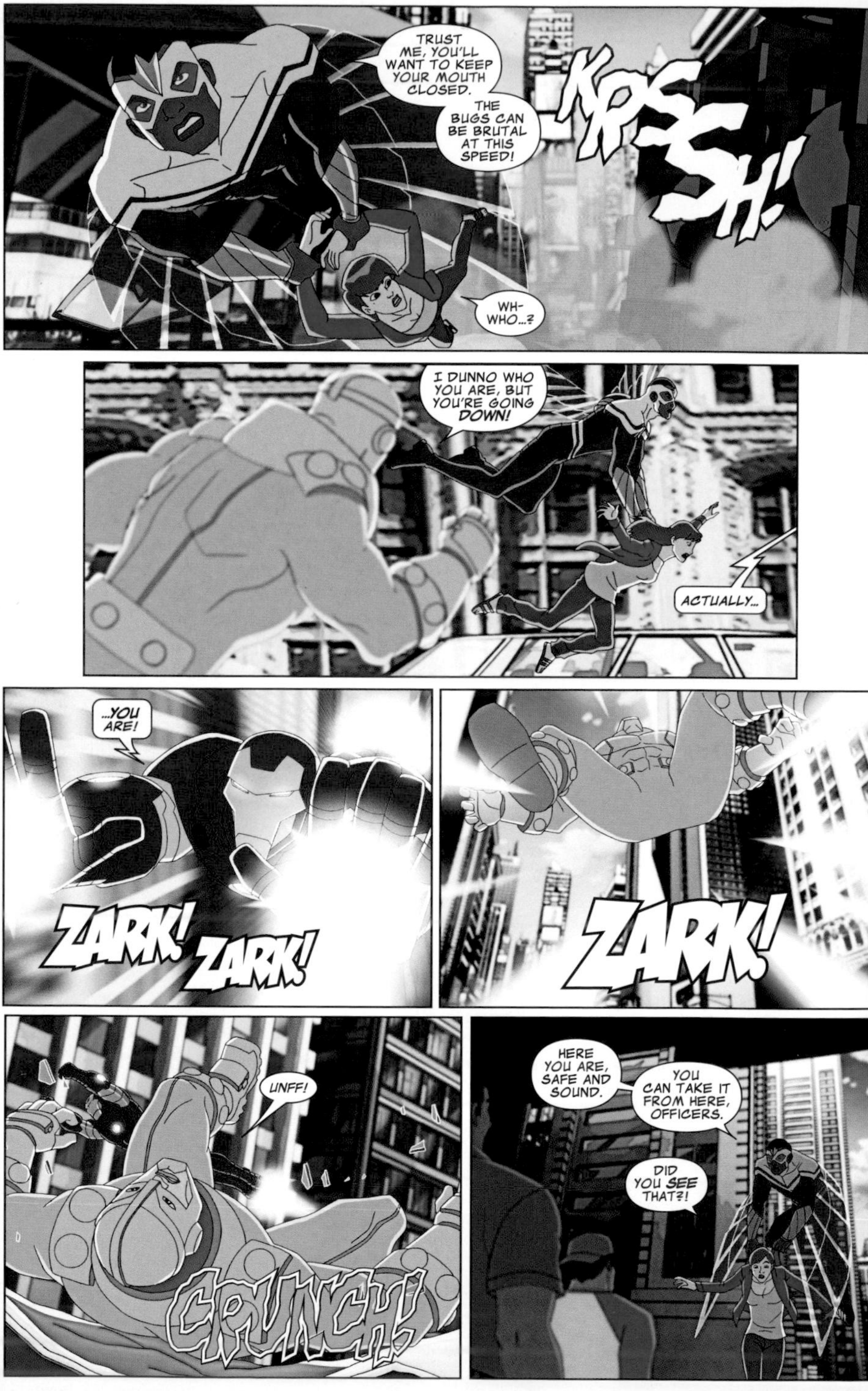
TRUST ME, YOU'LL WANT TO KEEP YOUR MOUTH CLOSED.
THE BUGS CAN BE BRUTAL AT THIS SPEED!
KRSSH!
WH- WHO...?
I DUNNO WHO YOU ARE, BUT YOU'RE GOING DOWN!
ACTUALLY...
...YOU ARE!
ZARK! ZARK!
ZARK!
UNFF!
CRUNCH!
HERE YOU ARE, SAFE AND SOUND.
YOU CAN TAKE IT FROM HERE, OFFICERS.
DID YOU SEE THAT?!

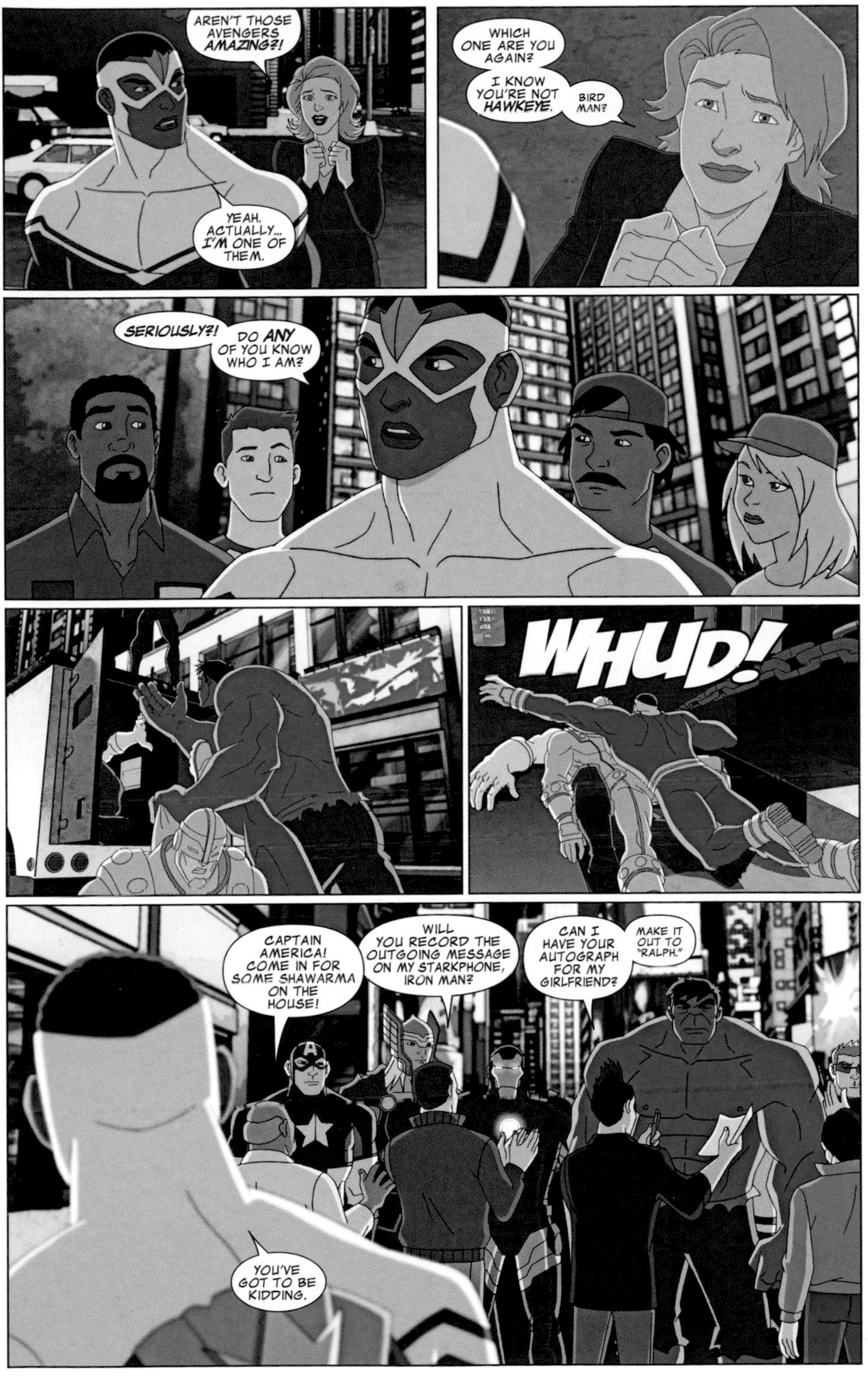
AREN'T THOSE AVENGERS AMAZING?!
YEAH. ACTUALLY... I'M ONE OF THEM.
WHICH ONE ARE YOU AGAIN?
I KNOW YOU'RE NOT HAWKEYE.
BIRD MAN?
SERIOUSLY?!
DO ANY OF YOU KNOW WHO I AM?
WHUD!
CAPTAIN AMERICA! COME IN FOR SOME SHAWARMA ON THE HOUSE!
WILL YOU RECORD THE OUTGOING MESSAGE ON MY STARKPHONE, IRON MAN?
CAN I HAVE YOUR AUTOGRAPH FOR MY GIRLFRIEND?
MAKE IT OUT TO "RALPH."
YOU'VE GOT TO BE KIDDING.

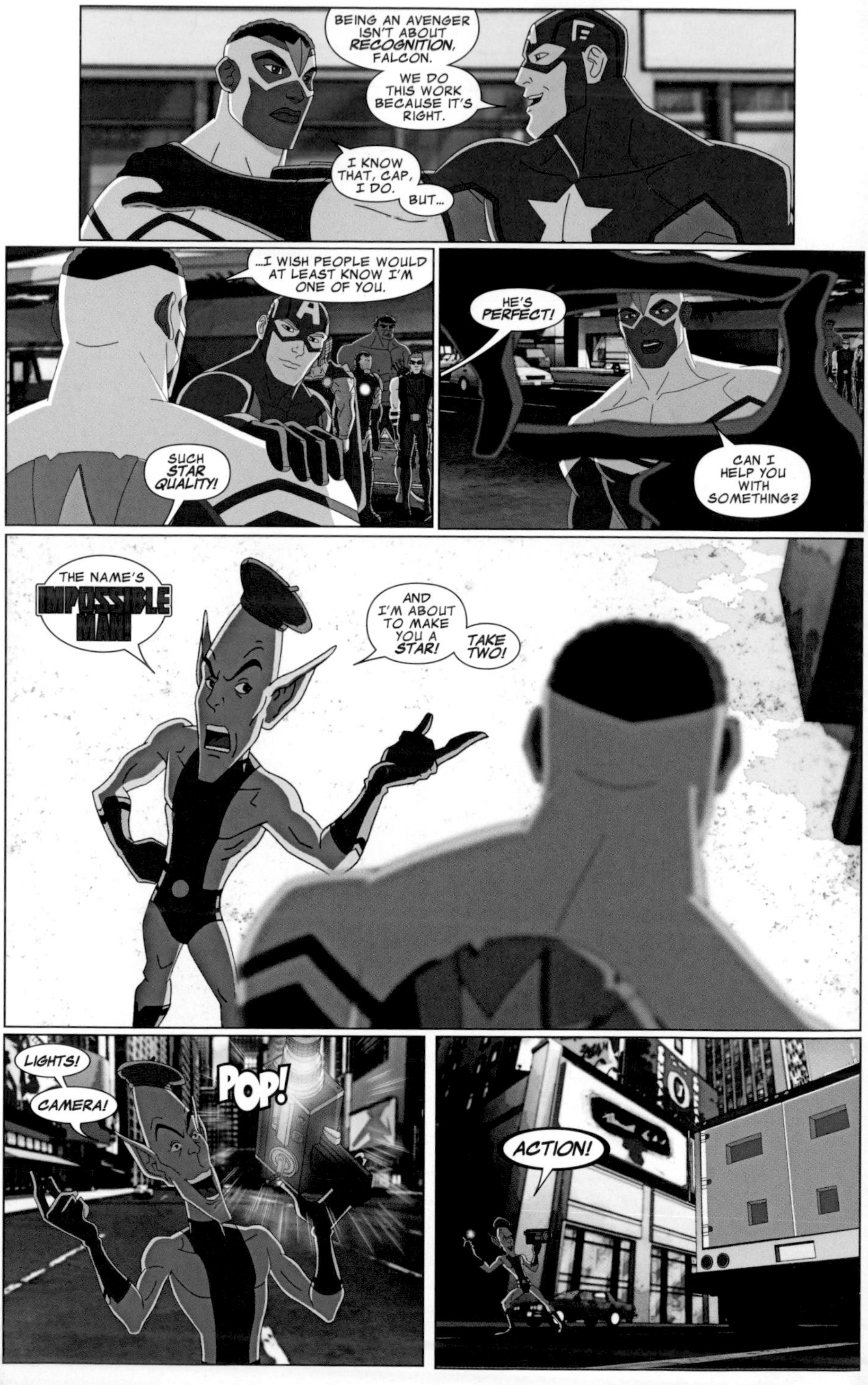
BEING AN AVENGER ISN'T ABOUT RECOGNITION, FALCON.
WE DO THIS WORK BECAUSE IT'S RIGHT.
I KNOW THAT, CAP, I DO.
BUT...
...I WISH PEOPLE WOULD AT LEAST KNOW I'M ONE OF YOU.
SUCH STAR QUALITY!
HE'S PERFECT!
CAN I HELP YOU WITH SOMETHING?
THE NAME'S IMPOSSIBLE MAN!
AND I'M ABOUT TO MAKE YOU A STAR!
TAKE TWO!
LIGHTS!
CAMERA!
POP!
ACTION!

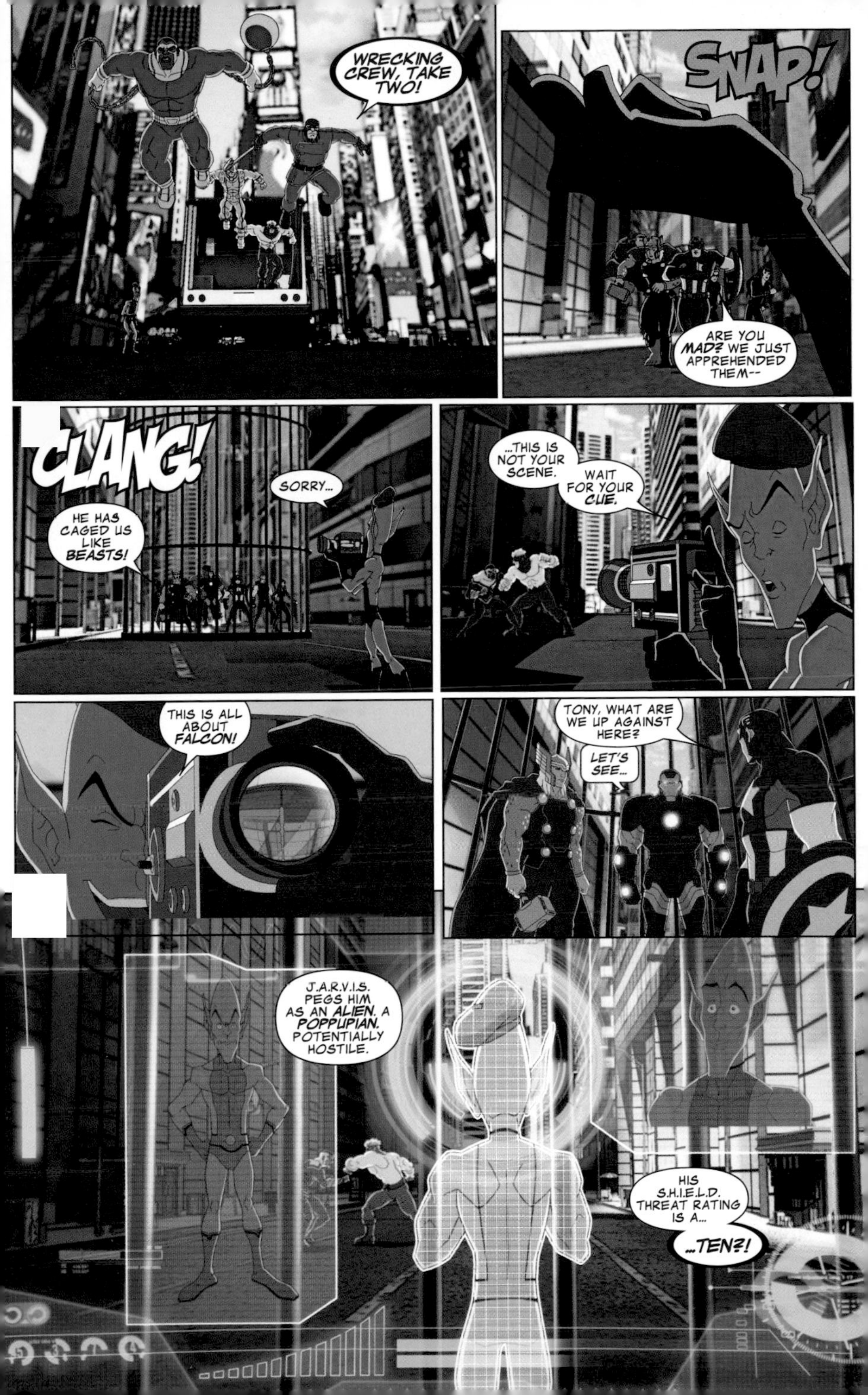
WRECKING CREW, TAKE TWO!
SNAP!
ARE YOU MAD? WE JUST APPREHENDED THEM--
CLANG!
HE HAS CAGED US LIKE BEASTS!
SORRY...
...THIS IS NOT YOUR SCENE.
WAIT FOR YOUR CUE.
THIS IS ALL ABOUT FALCON!
TONY, WHAT ARE WE UP AGAINST HERE?
LET'S SEE...
J.A.R.V.I.S. PEGS HIM AS AN ALIEN. A POPPUPIAN. POTENTIALLY HOSTILE.
HIS S.H.I.E.L.D. THREAT RATING IS A...
...TEN?!

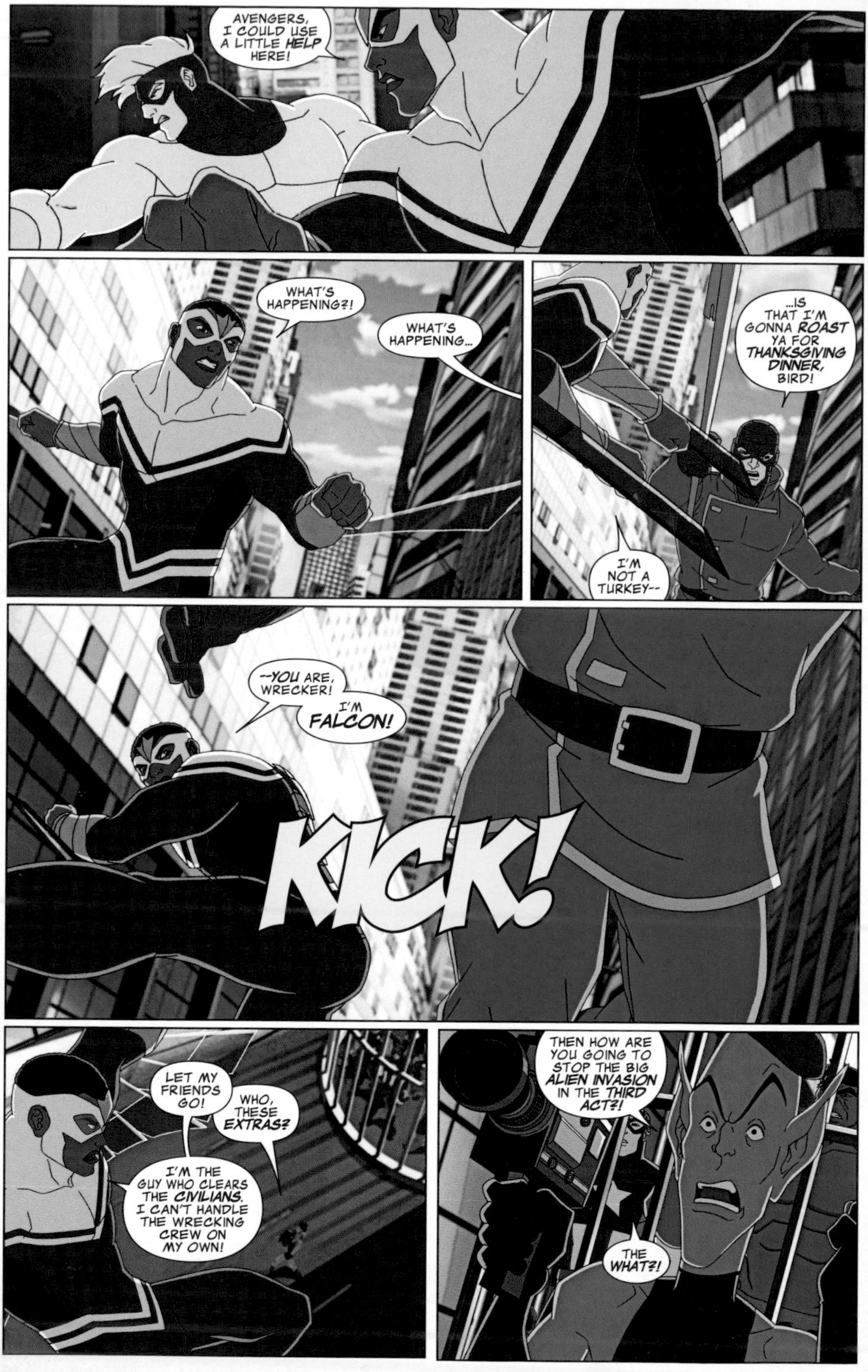
AVENGERS, I COULD USE A LITTLE HELP HERE!
WHAT'S HAPPENING?!
WHAT'S HAPPENING...
...IS THAT I'M GONNA ROAST YA FOR THANKSGIVING DINNER, BIRD!
I'M NOT A TURKEY--
--YOU ARE, WRECKER!
I'M FALCON!
KICK!
LET MY FRIENDS GO!
WHO, THESE EXTRAS?
I'M THE GUY WHO CLEARS THE CIVILIANS. I CAN'T HANDLE THE WRECKING CREW ON MY OWN!
THEN HOW ARE YOU GOING TO STOP THE BIG ALIEN INVASION IN THE THIRD ACT?!
THE WHAT?!

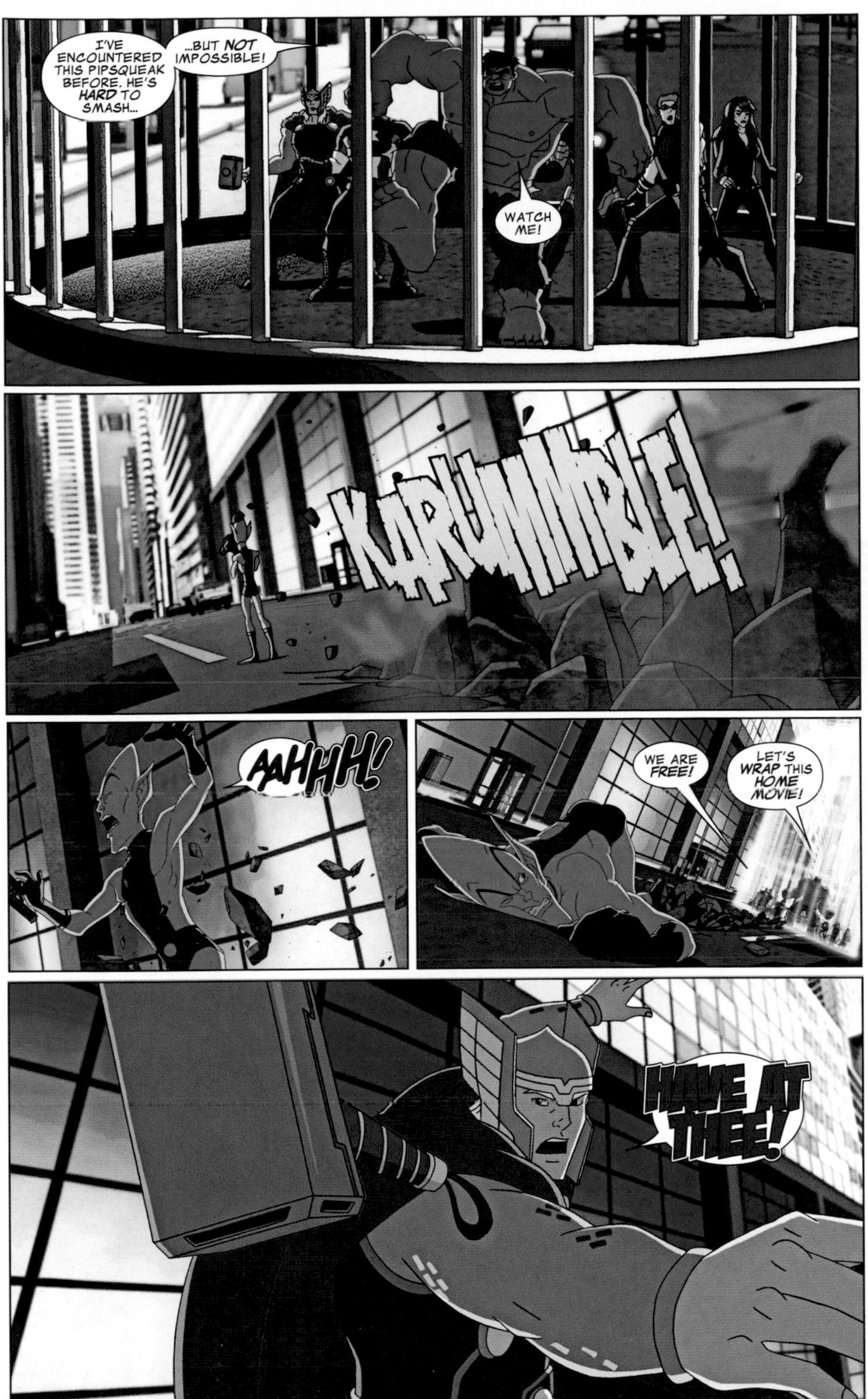
I'VE ENCOUNTERED THIS PIPSQUEAK BEFORE. HE'S HARD TO SMASH...
...BUT NOT IMPOSSIBLE!
WATCH ME!
KARUMMMBLE!
AAHHH!
WE ARE FREE!
LET'S WRAP THIS HOME MOVIE!
HAVE AT THEE!

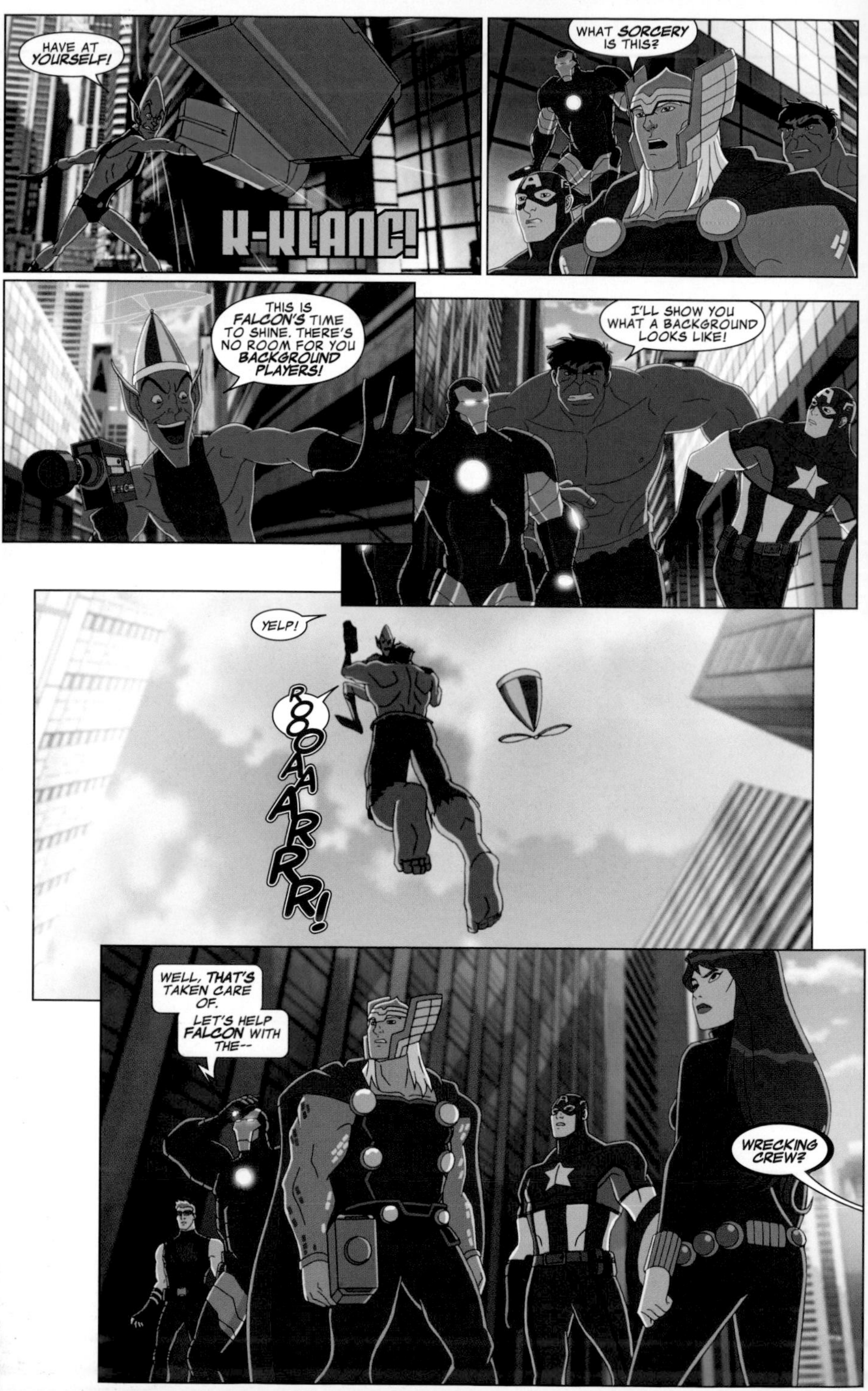
HAVE AT YOURSELF!
K-KLANG!
WHAT SORCERY IS THIS?
THIS IS FALCON'S TIME TO SHINE. THERE'S NO ROOM FOR YOU BACKGROUND PLAYERS!
I'LL SHOW YOU WHAT A BACKGROUND LOOKS LIKE!
YELP!
ROOOAAARRR!
WELL, THAT'S TAKEN CARE OF.
LET'S HELP FALCON WITH THE--
WRECKING CREW?

WHUD!

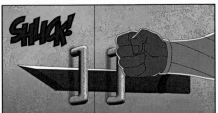

SHLICK!

CONSIDER THIS PRODUCTION WRAPPED.

IMPRESSIVE, FALCON. YOUR ALIEN FRIEND IS RIGHT ABOUT YOU.

YOU'VE GOT STAR QUALITY!

THANKS, TONY, BUT... WHEN IT COMES TO THE AVENGERS, I'M JUST AN EXTRA.

MMHHH!

CRASH!

HHRRPPPFF!

AH! MY CAMERA!

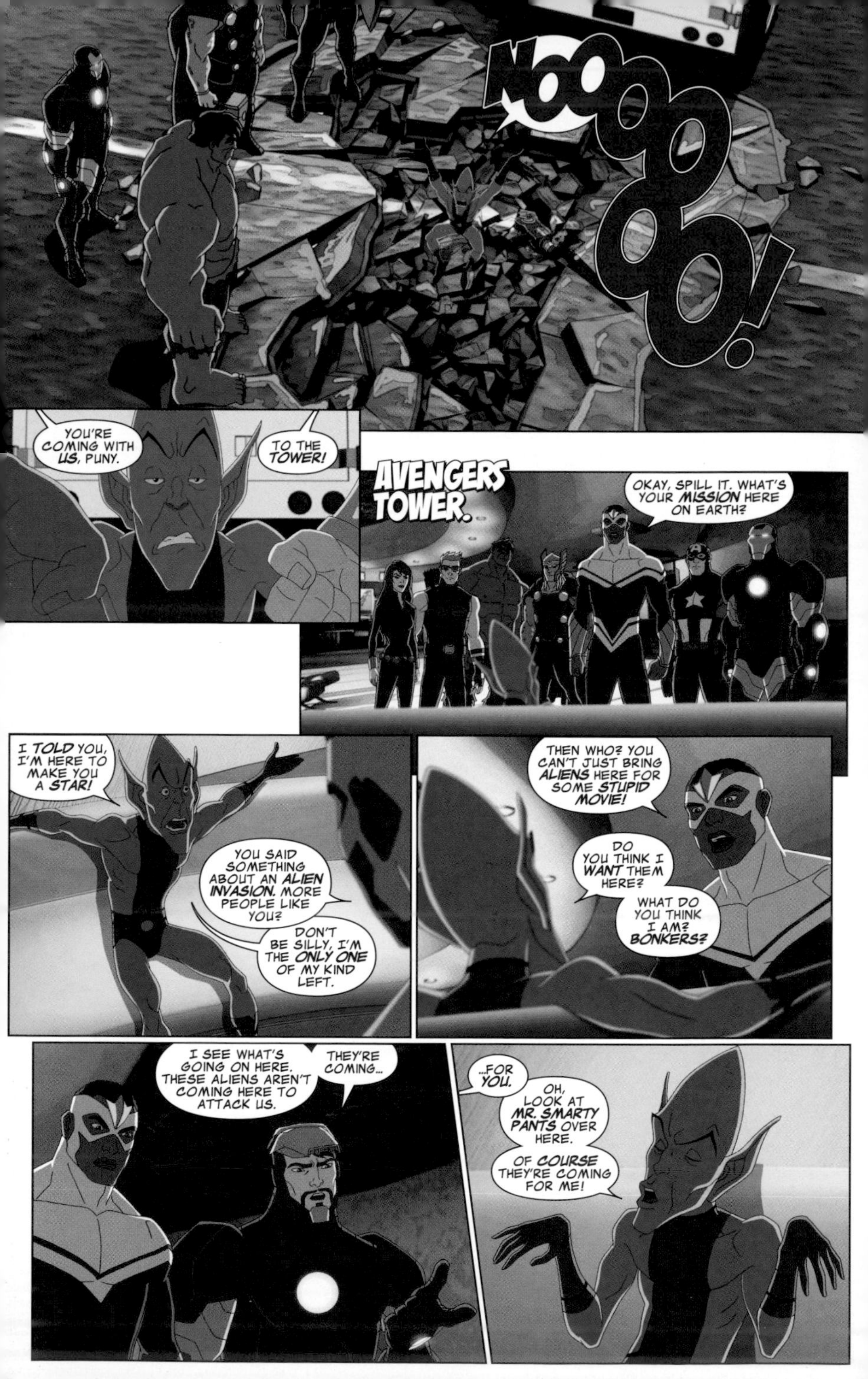
NOOOOOOO!
YOU'RE COMING WITH US, PUNY.
TO THE TOWER!
AVENGERS TOWER.
OKAY, SPILL IT. WHAT'S YOUR MISSION HERE ON EARTH?
I TOLD YOU, I'M HERE TO MAKE YOU A STAR!
YOU SAID SOMETHING ABOUT AN ALIEN INVASION. MORE PEOPLE LIKE YOU?
DON'T BE SILLY, I'M THE ONLY ONE OF MY KIND LEFT.
THEN WHO? YOU CAN'T JUST BRING ALIENS HERE FOR SOME STUPID MOVIE!
DO YOU THINK I WANT THEM HERE?
WHAT DO YOU THINK I AM? BONKERS?
I SEE WHAT'S GOING ON HERE. THESE ALIENS AREN'T COMING HERE TO ATTACK US.
THEY'RE COMING...
...FOR YOU.
OH, LOOK AT MR. SMARTY PANTS OVER HERE.
OF COURSE THEY'RE COMING FOR ME!

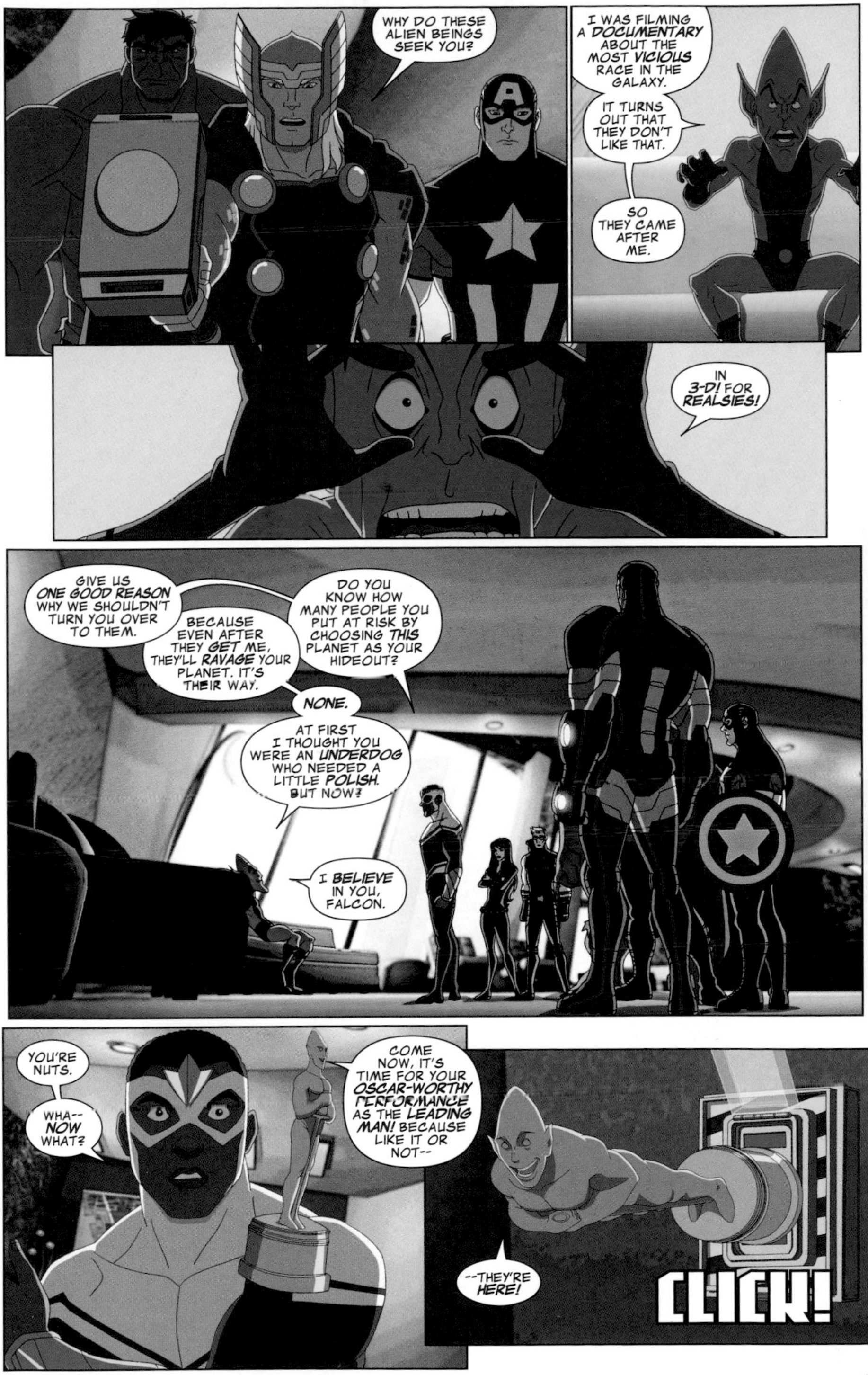
WHY DO THESE ALIEN BEINGS SEEK YOU?
I WAS FILMING A DOCUMENTARY ABOUT THE MOST VICIOUS RACE IN THE GALAXY.
IT TURNS OUT THAT THEY DON'T LIKE THAT.
SO THEY CAME AFTER ME.
IN 3-D! FOR REALSIES!
GIVE US ONE GOOD REASON WHY WE SHOULDN'T TURN YOU OVER TO THEM.
BECAUSE EVEN AFTER THEY GET ME, THEY'LL RAVAGE YOUR PLANET. IT'S THEIR WAY.
DO YOU KNOW HOW MANY PEOPLE YOU PUT AT RISK BY CHOOSING THIS PLANET AS YOUR HIDEOUT?
NONE.
AT FIRST I THOUGHT YOU WERE AN UNDERDOG WHO NEEDED A LITTLE POLISH. BUT NOW?
I BELIEVE IN YOU, FALCON.
YOU'RE NUTS.
WHA-- NOW WHAT?
COME NOW, IT'S TIME FOR YOUR OSCAR-WORTHY PERFORMANCE AS THE LEADING MAN! BECAUSE LIKE IT OR NOT--
--THEY'RE HERE!
CLICK!

WHRRR

LET'S MAKE A MOVIE!

ACTION!

ꭷꭶꮎ ꭶꭱꭴ ꮲꮻꭲꮑꮎ ꭴꮑꭶ ꮎꭷꮎ ꮰꭱꮣ ꮻꭷꭷꮲ ꭴꭶ ꮼꮣꮎꭶ ꮼꭴ ꮄꮲꮗ!

WANT TO KNOW WHAT HE'S SAYING, HEROES? CHECK THE BACK PAGE! --S.H.I.E.L.D. AGENT CARAMAGNA.

"PLEASE TELL ME THAT'S NOT THE *CHITAURI*."

I DON'T STAND A *CHANCE* AGAINST *THESE* GUYS!

YOU DON'T HAVE TO. THE AVENGERS ARE ALL ABOUT *TEAMWORK*.

IN THAT CASE--

--AVENGERS ASSEMBLE!

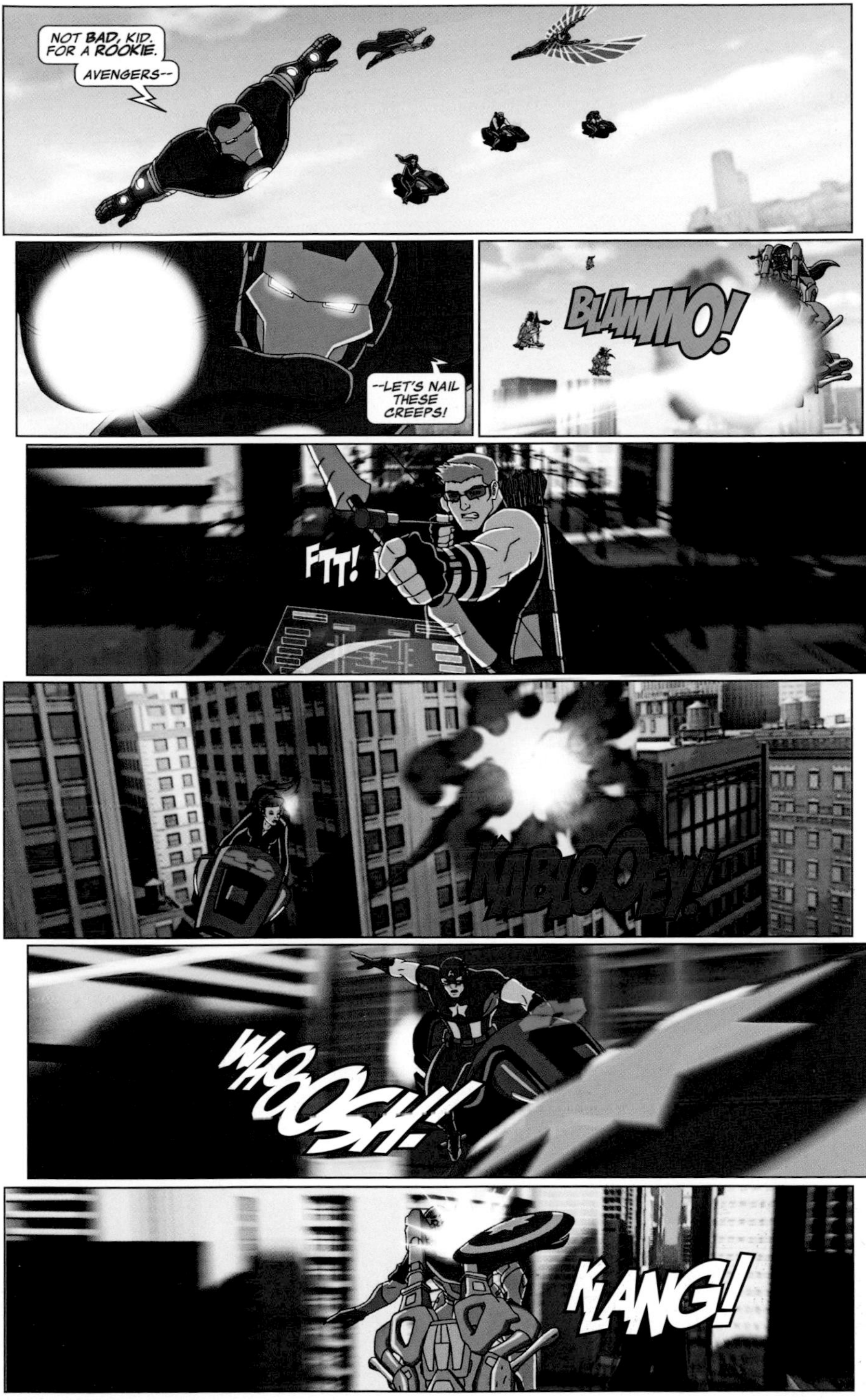
NOT BAD, KID. FOR A ROOKIE.
AVENGERS--
--LET'S NAIL THESE CREEPS!
BLAMMO!
FTT!
KABLOOEY!!
WHOOSH!!
KLANG!

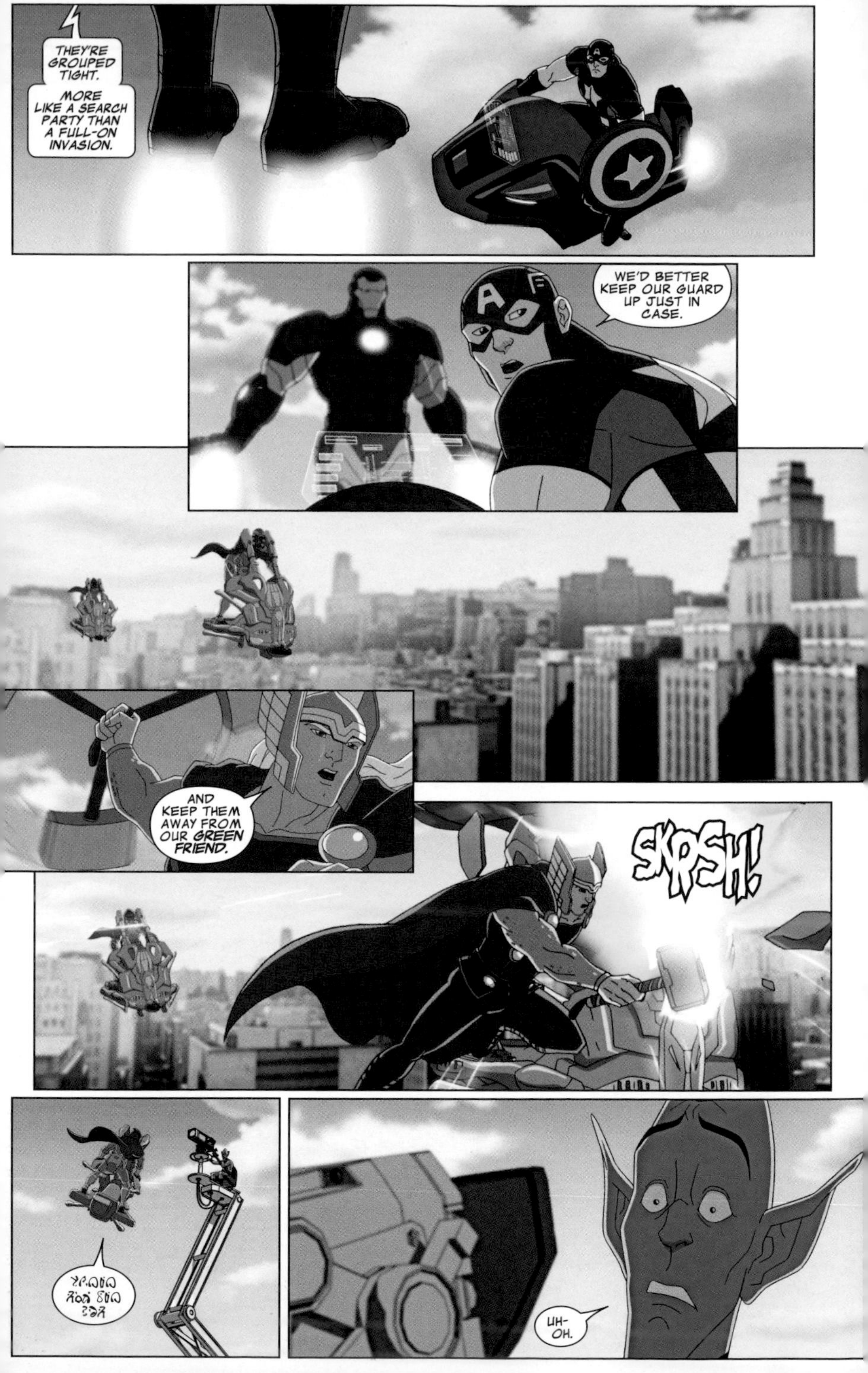
THEY'RE GROUPED TIGHT.
MORE LIKE A SEARCH PARTY THAN A FULL-ON INVASION.
WE'D BETTER KEEP OUR GUARD UP JUST IN CASE.
AND KEEP THEM AWAY FROM OUR GREEN FRIEND.
SKRSH!
UH-OH.

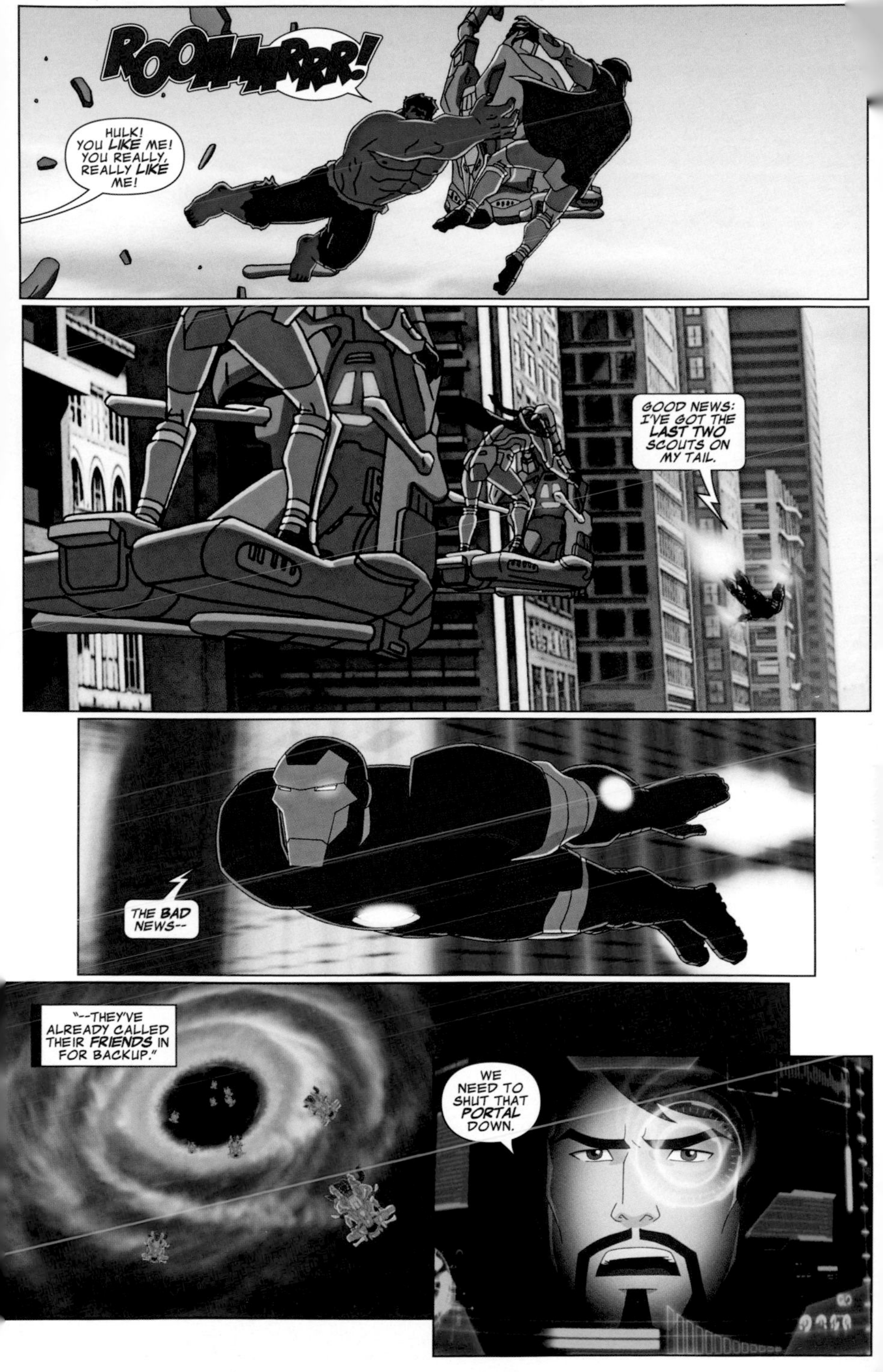
ROOAARRR!
HULK! YOU LIKE ME! YOU REALLY, REALLY LIKE ME!
GOOD NEWS: I'VE GOT THE LAST TWO SCOUTS ON MY TAIL.
THE BAD NEWS--
"--THEY'VE ALREADY CALLED THEIR FRIENDS IN FOR BACKUP."
WE NEED TO SHUT THAT PORTAL DOWN.

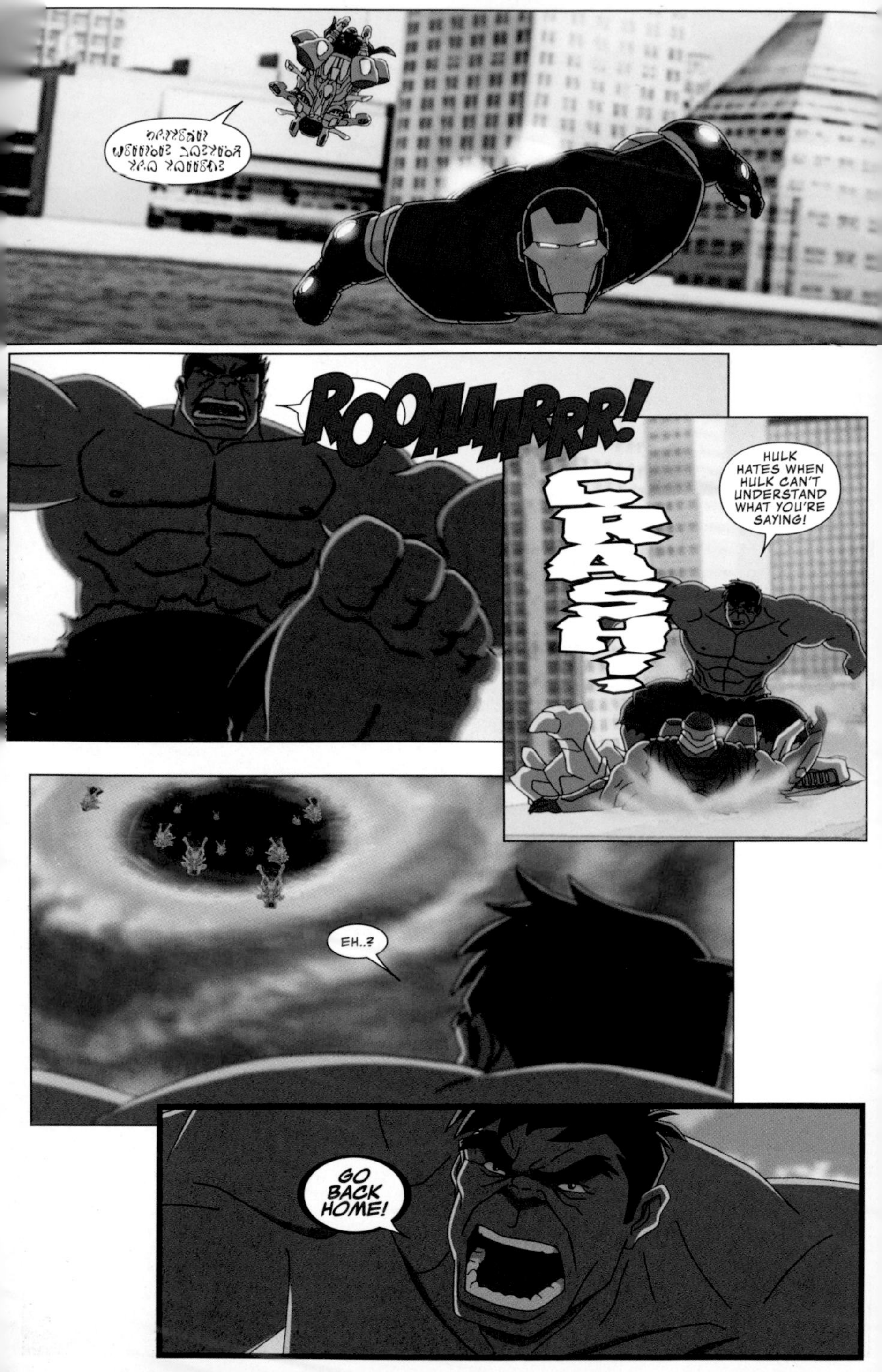
ROOAAARRR!
CRASH!
HULK HATES WHEN HULK CAN'T UNDERSTAND WHAT YOU'RE SAYING!
EH..?
GO BACK HOME!

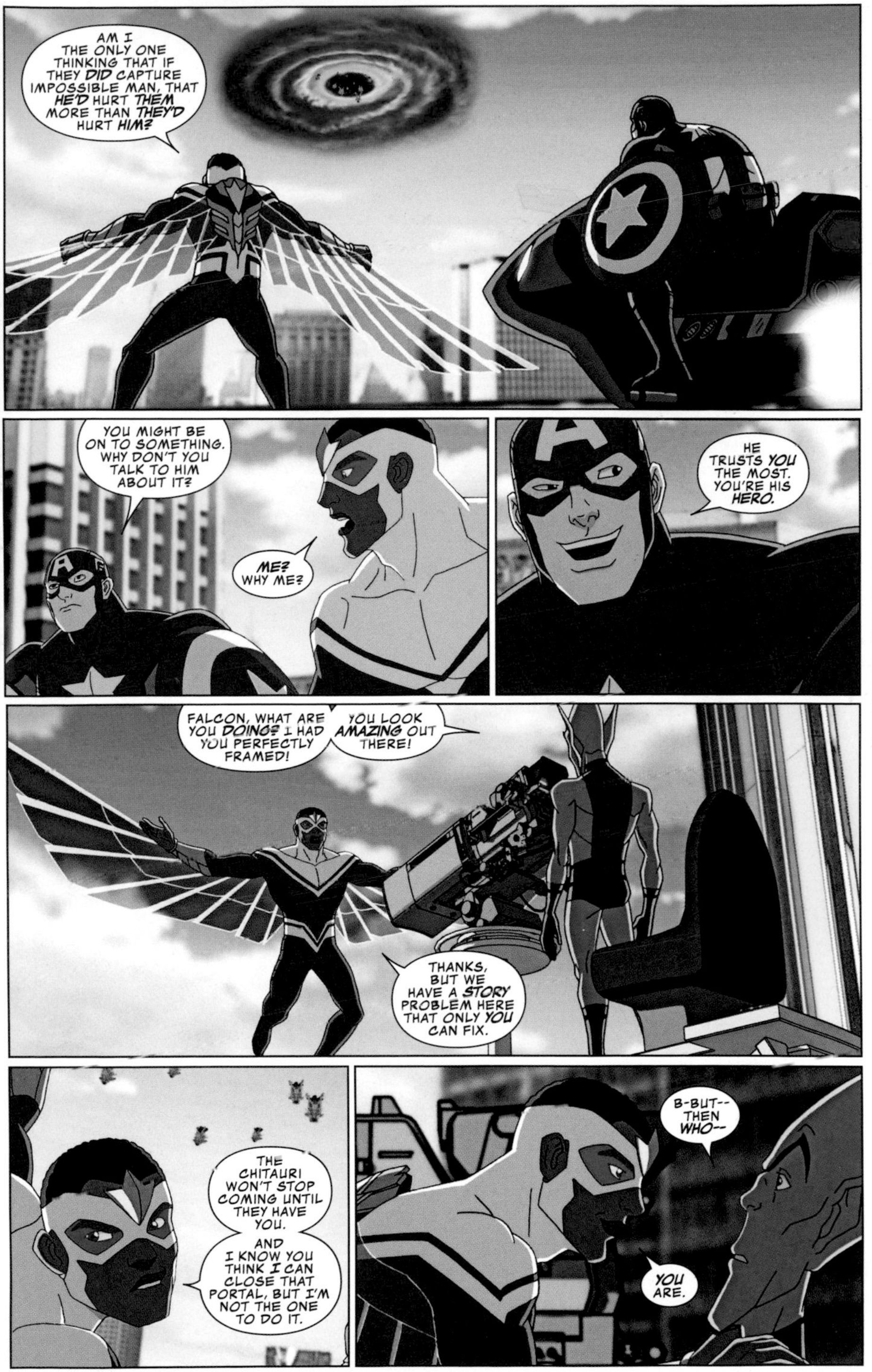
AM I THE ONLY ONE THINKING THAT IF THEY DID CAPTURE IMPOSSIBLE MAN, THAT HE'D HURT THEM MORE THAN THEY'D HURT HIM?
YOU MIGHT BE ON TO SOMETHING. WHY DON'T YOU TALK TO HIM ABOUT IT?
ME? WHY ME?
HE TRUSTS YOU THE MOST. YOU'RE HIS HERO.
FALCON, WHAT ARE YOU DOING? I HAD YOU PERFECTLY FRAMED!
YOU LOOK AMAZING OUT THERE!
THANKS, BUT WE HAVE A STORY PROBLEM HERE THAT ONLY YOU CAN FIX.
THE CHITAURI WON'T STOP COMING UNTIL THEY HAVE YOU.
AND I KNOW YOU THINK I CAN CLOSE THAT PORTAL, BUT I'M NOT THE ONE TO DO IT.
B-BUT-- THEN WHO--
YOU ARE.

ME?!

YOU HAVE THE POWER TO SEND THEM ALL FAR, FAR AWAY.

THIRD ACT TWIST. IMPOSSIBLE GALACTIC SPACE TELEPORTATION MISSILE.

WE'LL GET YOU TO THE RIFT. YOU SCATTER THE BAD GUYS ACROSS UNKNOWN DIMENSIONS AND SPLIT JUST ONE OF YOUR ATOMS WHILE YOU SHAPE-SHIFT TO BLOW THE RIFT CLOSED.

SAVE THE UNIVERSE? ME? NO ONE'S EVER ASKED ME TO DO THAT BEFORE.

I ACCEPT!

BWOM!

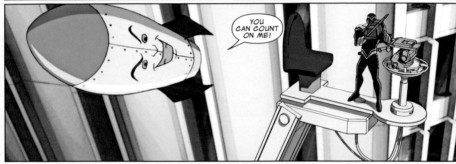

YOU CAN COUNT ON ME!

LET'S DO THIS!

IRON MAN, I NEED A JET ASSIST!

ON IT!

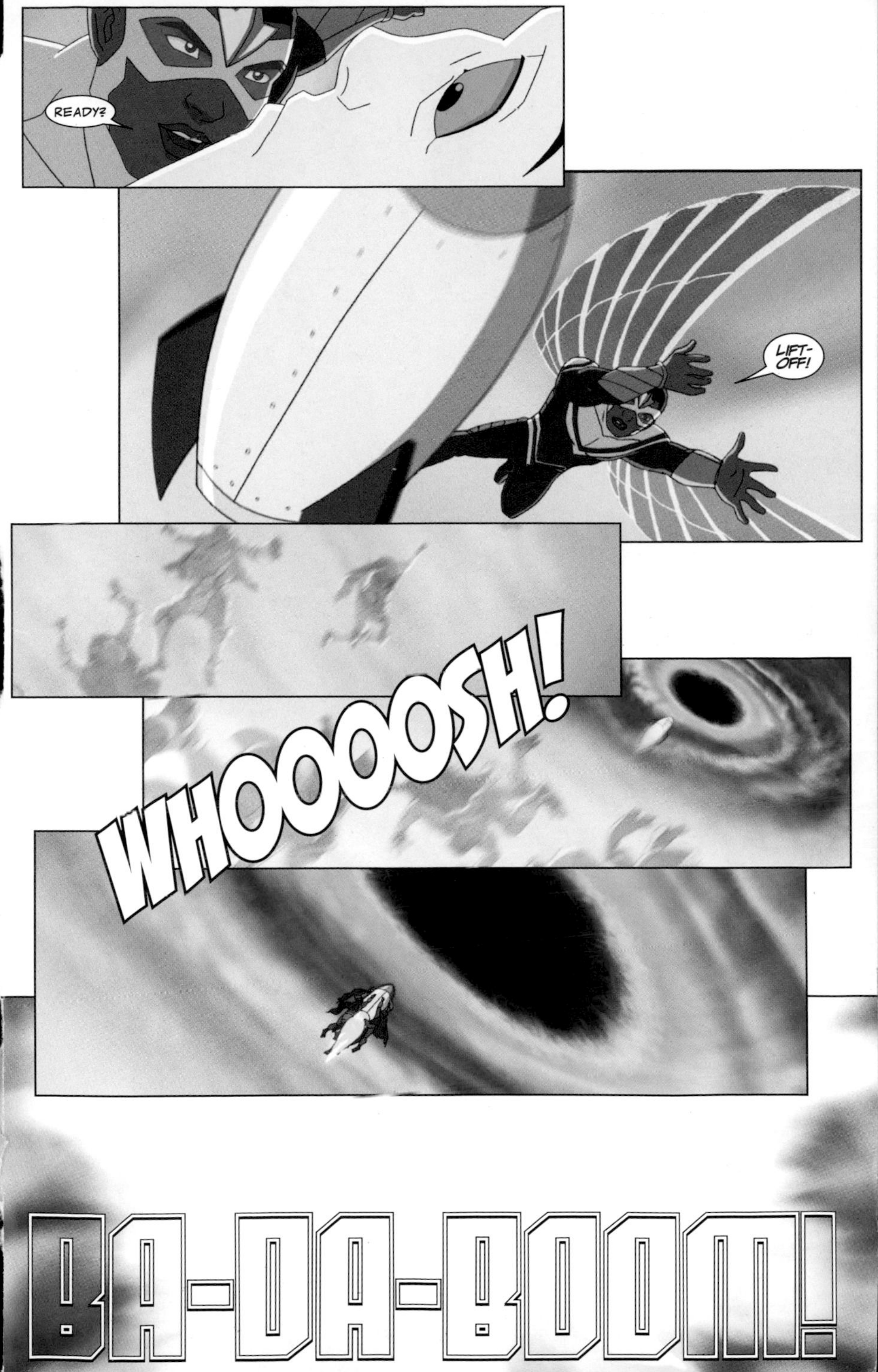
READY?
LIFT-OFF!
WHOOOOSH!
BA-DA-BOOM!

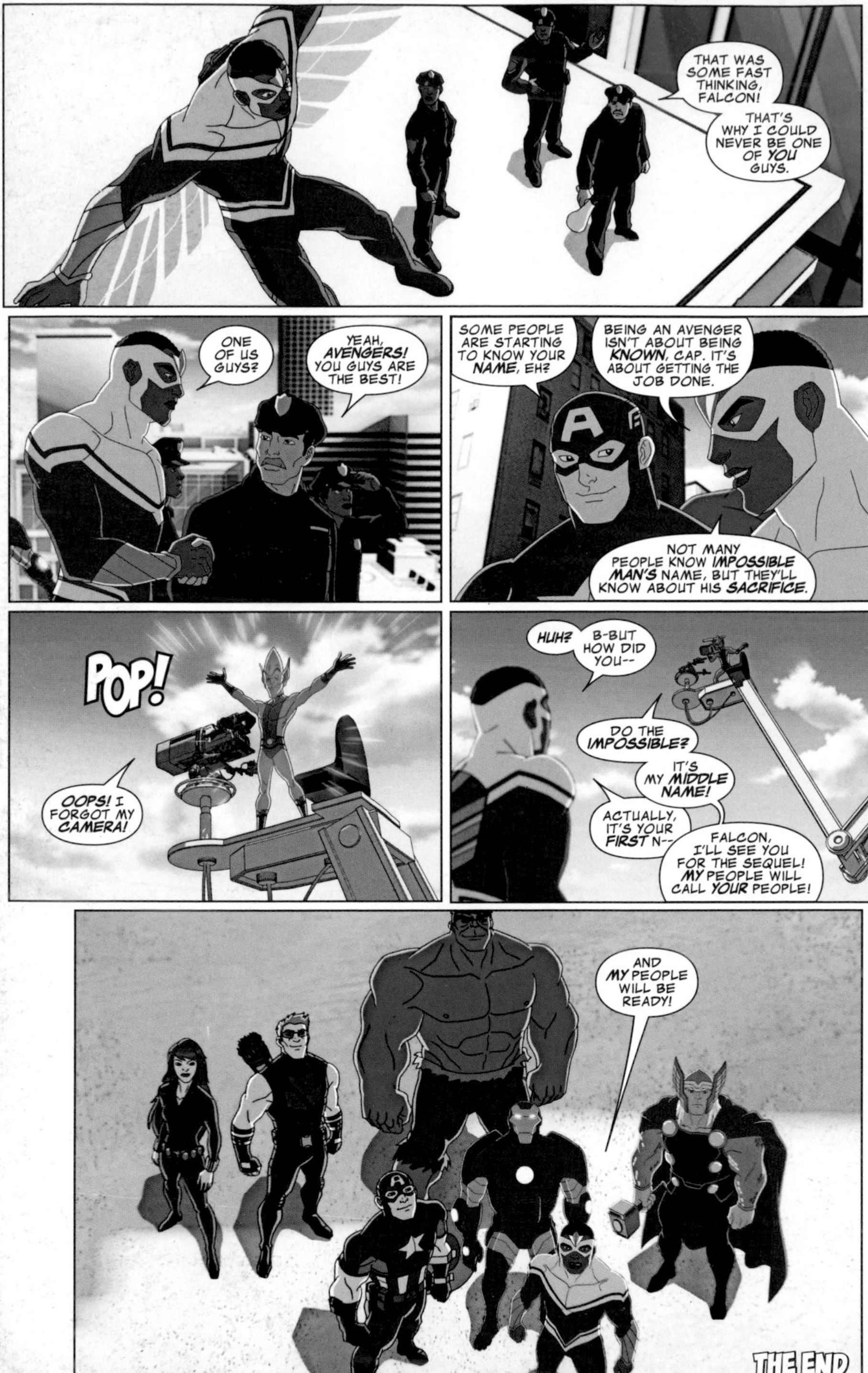
THAT WAS SOME FAST THINKING, FALCON!
THAT'S WHY I COULD NEVER BE ONE OF YOU GUYS.
ONE OF US GUYS?
YEAH, AVENGERS! YOU GUYS ARE THE BEST!
SOME PEOPLE ARE STARTING TO KNOW YOUR NAME, EH?
BEING AN AVENGER ISN'T ABOUT BEING KNOWN, CAP. IT'S ABOUT GETTING THE JOB DONE.
NOT MANY PEOPLE KNOW IMPOSSIBLE MAN'S NAME, BUT THEY'LL KNOW ABOUT HIS SACRIFICE.
POP!
OOPS! I FORGOT MY CAMERA!
HUH?
B-BUT HOW DID YOU--
DO THE IMPOSSIBLE?
IT'S MY MIDDLE NAME!
ACTUALLY, IT'S YOUR FIRST N--
FALCON, I'LL SEE YOU FOR THE SEQUEL! MY PEOPLE WILL CALL YOUR PEOPLE!
AND MY PEOPLE WILL BE READY!
THE END